A HOUSE FOR MY NAME
QUESTIONS & ANSWERS

JOSHUA APPEL

canonpress
Moscow, Idaho

This question and answer guide is designed to be used with Peter J. Leithart's, *A House for My Name: A Survey of the Old Testament* (Moscow: Canon Press, 2000).

Published by Canon Press
P.O. Box 8729, Moscow, ID 83843
800.488.2034 | www.canonpress.com

Joshua Appel, *A House for My Name: Questions & Answers*
Copyright © 2010 by Canon Press.

Cover and interior design by Laura Storm.
Printed in the United States of America.

Library of Congress Cataloging-in-Publication Data

Appel, Joshua.
  A house for My name : questions & answers / Joshua Appel.
    p. cm.
  ISBN-13: 978-1-59128-063-7 (pbk.)
  ISBN-10: 1-59128-063-X (pbk.)
  1. Bible. O.T.--Miscellanea. I. Leithart, Peter J. House for My name. II. Title.
  BS1194.L39 2000 Suppl.
  221.6'1--dc22
                                    2009005321

10 11 12 13 14 15   7 6 5 4 3 2 1

CONTENTS

CHAPTER I
BOOK OF BEGINNINGS
5

CHAPTER 2
OUT OF EGYPT HAVE I CALLED MY SON
19

CHAPTER 3
FROM SINAI TO SHILOH
33

CHAPTER 4
THE HOUSE OF DAVID
AND THE HOUSE OF YAHWEH
53

CHAPTER 5
WALKING IN THE CUSTOMS OF THE NATIONS
71

CHAPTER 6
THE LAST DAYS OF JUDAH
83

CHAPTER 7
EXILE AND NEW EXODUS
91

CHAPTER 8
ISRAEL DEAD AND REBORN
103

BOOK OF BEGINNINGS

Three-Story House: *Genesis 1:1–2:4*

REVIEW QUESTIONS [pages 43–49]

1. How is the world like a house?

Just like a house, the world has "foundations" (Deut. 32:22; 2 Sam. 22:8, 16; Ps. 104:5) which support the earth and the heavens, which are spread out as the ceiling of a tent (Is. 40:22). Throughout the Bible (Job 38:4–7; 9:6; 26:11; Ps. 77:16–18) this kind of building language is used to describe God's creation.

2. How do the first three days of creation match the second three days?

God takes six days to build His house. During the first three days, God makes a three-storied house by dividing one thing from another. The first day He divides the light from the darkness; the second day He divides the waters in heaven from the waters on the earth and puts the sky in-between; and the third day He divides the dry land from the sea. The final three days, God fills up the house He made. On the fourth day, God creates the sun, moon, and stars to rule over the day and night. On the fifth day, God creates birds to fly in the open space of heaven and fish to swim in the waters. And finally on the sixth day, God finishes His creation by making animals and man to live on the dry land.

3. What are the stories of God's three-story house?

The Bible mentions this three-story house many times. In the second commandment, God forbids us to bow down to an image of anything in "heaven above, or on the earth beneath, or in the waters under the earth" (Exod. 20:4). Above is the sky, what the Bible calls the "firmament of heaven," which is stretched out as "tent curtain" (Is. 40:22). Below are the waters "beneath the earth" (Exod. 20:4). In between is the dry land. Sometimes when the Bible mentions the three-story house, it's not as obvious as it is in the second commandment.

4. What is Psalm 77 talking about? Why does it describe this event as if it were the end of the world?

Psalm 77 is talking about Israel's exodus from Egypt (vv. 19–20). The psalmist describes this event as though it were the end of the world because the Exodus is a world-shaking event. When God shakes the world, it signifies that He is bringing an old world to an end (e.g., Pharaoh and the bondage of Egypt) and at the same time, bringing a new "creation" into being (Heb. 12:26–27).

5. How does Hannah's song compare Israel to a house?

First Samuel 2:8 describes the "pillars of the earth" as supporting the "house" of Israel (also see Ps. 75:3). In this passage, Israel as a nation is described as a three-storied universe. Hannah is looking forward to a time when the wicked rulers (i.e., "pillars") would be replaced by the righteous. Samson does this very thing when he brings down the "house" of Dagon by destroying its "pillars" (Judg. 16:23–31).

6. What do the sun, moon, and stars represent? What is Isaiah talking about when he describes heavenly bodies falling from the sky?

The sun, moon, and stars, which are located in the "upper room" of the universe, often symbolize the kings and rulers of the earth. Thus, cataclysmic language (such as that used in Isaiah 13:9–10) can be used to describe the end of a geopolitical world (i.e., Babylon) rather than the literal end of the entire universe.

7. What does the land often represent? What is the sea?

Often the land represents Israel and the sea represents the Gentile nations (Ps. 46:1–3, 6; 65:7–8; Is. 8:6–8; Jer. 51:34–42).

8. How does Isaiah describe the Assyrian invasion of Judah?

Isaiah 8:6–8 describes the Assyrian invasion of Judah as a river threatening to overflow its banks and flood the land. Because Israel rejected the "river whose streams make glad the city of God" (Ps. 46:4), God allowed the "Euphrates" to overflow and engulf the land of Judah. This imagery reminds us of Noah's flood. Judgment is pictured in the collapse of the ordained boundary between land and sea (Gen. 1:9)

9. How does Jeremiah describe Nebuchadnezzar and Babylon?

Jeremiah describes Nebuchadnezzar, the Babylonian emperor, as a sea monster who devours Israel (Jer. 51:34–35). In the verses following Jeremiah 51:35, the Lord says He will judge Babylon and punish Bel, a Babylonian god, by making him vomit Israel back into the land.

THOUGHT QUESTIONS

1. What does Psalm 82:5 mean by "the foundations of the earth"?

Psalm 82 describes God's judgment upon the rulers of the nations. Throughout the psalm, the rulers are equated with their divinities (vv. 1, 6). The rulers are related to their gods and are the "pillars" of their kingdoms. Therefore, when they are judged, "all the foundations of the earth are shaken."

2. Compare Genesis 1:2 and Genesis 8:1. Note that the word for "Spirit" is the same as the word for "wind." In light of this, explain what's happening in Genesis 8:1.

In Genesis 1:2, the creation of the heavens and the earth is identified with the Spirit of God "moving over the surface of the waters." The use of this same imagery in Genesis 8:1 shows us that God is recreating the earth after the judgment of the flood. Genesis 8:1 marks a new beginning for God's creation.

3. Notice the references to the three-story house in Revelation 8:1–13. Notice also that there are seven trumpets being sounded. Explain how this connects to Genesis 1.

Revelation 8:1–13 describes God's judgment on the earth in a way that mirrors the three-story structure of creation in Genesis 1. When the angels sound their trumpets, judgments occur on the earth (v. 7), the sea, (vv. 8–9), the springs of waters (vv. 10–11), and in the heavens (v. 12). This means that God's judgment is a great reversal of creation.

4. Why is it significant that Noah's ark has three levels (Gen. 6:16)?

In the midst of the great flood, Noah's three-leveled ark is a mini universe that preserves creation from destruction. When the flood subsides, a "new" creation is replenished by the world that was saved in Noah's ark.

5. If the land pictures Israel, what do land animals represent? Look at Psalms 77:20 and 80:1.

Both Psalms 77:20 and 80:1 use the imagery of sacrificial land animals (flocks and herds), especially sheep, to picture Israel. Other clean land animals often represent Gentile God-fearers who live within Israel.

Junior Architects:
Genesis 1:26–28; 2:1–25; 6–9

REVIEW QUESTIONS [pages 50–57]

1. What does it mean for Adam to be the "image" of God?

Genesis 1:26–27 says that God made man in His "image and likeness." An image is a copy. Thus, Adam and Eve were to copy God's work as they "subdued" creation as His representatives. Just as God fashioned creation into a glorious "house," so Adam was to be a builder too. This purpose is reflected in God's command to be fruitful and multiply, to fill the earth and subdue it.

2. What does "subdue" mean? What is Adam supposed to "subdue"? What is the result supposed to be?

In the Old Testament, the word "subdue" is used to describe victory at war as well as "subduing" people into slavery (Jer. 34:11, 16; 2 Chr. 28:10). Before the Fall, "subduing" the creation meant that Adam would have to work hard to rule creation. He was to discover new ways to use what God had made and bring it into the service of man through wise stewardship. Adam was also to "subdue" creation by making it pleasing to God; he was to raise faithful children who worshiped and served the Lord. By doing this, Adam was to create a house for God within the house God had made for him.

3. Describe the map of the original creation in Genesis 2.

In Genesis 2:11–13, creation is divided into three areas: the Garden (situated to the east in Eden), the land of Eden, and the larger world.

4. In what part of the land of Eden is the Garden? Why is this significant?

Genesis 2:8 says that the Garden was in the east of Eden. After the Fall, the Lord stationed cherubim at the entrance of the Garden, which is in the east (Gen. 3:24). From this point on, traveling east is always traveling away from the presence of the Lord (and the Garden) while traveling west is moving toward Him. This also shows us that Adam was meant to move out of the Garden to govern the surrounding land as he moved closer to the Lord.

5. How do we know that the Garden was on a mountain? Give some examples of how this appears later in the Bible.

Genesis 2:10 says that the river flows from the land of Eden though the Garden. While Eden is higher, the Garden itself must have been located on high ground. In Ezekiel 28:12–14 the prophet announces judgment against Tyre and describes the "prince of Tyre" as an Adam who is in the Garden of God (v. 13). Significantly, in the next verse (v. 14) Ezekiel equates the Garden with "the holy mountain of God."

Additionally, in the period between the destruction of the tabernacle and the building of the temple, Samuel conducts worship at Ramah which means "high place" (cf. 1 Sam. 7:17). Later, David brings the ark to Jerusalem and puts it in a tent on Mount Zion, and Solomon builds the Lord's temple on the same mountain in Jerusalem.

6. What is Adam's job in the Garden?

Adam was to serve the Lord and guard the Garden. Both of these duties point to the priests' responsibility to "guard" the Lord's house and offer the "service" of worship, the same words used to describe Adam's duties in Genesis 2:15 (cf. Exod. 20:5; Num. 8:15; Deut. 7:4). When the Lord divided the world into the Garden and the world, He added corresponding "kingly" duties to Adam's commission. In the Garden, Adam met with God, worshiped Him, and protected the Garden from intruders (priestly duties), while he was to subdue the world and rule over it (kingly duties).

7. In what ways is Adam's sin a failure to be a priest?

Adam failed in his priestly duty to guard the Garden from the lying accusations of the serpent. Instead of protecting

Eve, Adam stood by and allowed Satan's words to go un-challenged. His failure to protect the Garden resulted in his willingness to serve the serpent rather than the Lord, which made him a servant rather than a king in his own house.

8. What is the difference between Cain's sin and Adam's? Between Cain's sin and the sin of the "sons of God"?

Adam's sin is in the Garden and has to do with worship; Cain's sin is in the field (the land) and has to do with a brother; and the sons of God sin by marrying the daughters of men (unbelievers) in the world. Thus, sin spreads from the Garden, to the land, to the whole world until it engulfs the entire creation.

9. Explain how the flood is a "reversal" of creation.

After sin had corrupted the original creation, God reverses creation by sending a flood to wipe out all that He had made. Waters again come to "cover the earth" and prepare the way for a "new" creation.

10. How is Noah a new Adam? In what ways does Noah advance beyond Adam?

Like Adam, Noah is told to be "fruitful and to multiply and fill the earth" (Gen. 9:1). God also promises that Noah and his descendants will have dominion over the animals (Gen. 9:2), but God extends Noah's authority by giving him the responsibility to execute murderers (Gen. 9:5–6). Instead of being given a garden, Noah plants a vineyard and his narrative ends with him at peace enjoying the fruit of his labor (Gen. 9:20–21). Noah has been delivered from the violence of the flood to rest in the peace of a "new" Sabbath.

THOUGHT QUESTIONS

1. Read Ephesians 1:21–23, noticing how Paul refers to Genesis 1:26–28. What is Paul telling us about Jesus?

Paul is telling us that Jesus is a new (and final!) Adam who was raised from the dead and is seated at the right hand of the Father as the Lord of all creation. He is the head over all things and every power has been brought into subjection under His feet. According to Paul, Jesus "fills all things," fulfilling the Lord's command to Adam to "fill the earth." Jesus is also a faithful husband to His bride, the Church. In Him Adam's responsibilities as priest and king have been fulfilled.

2. Read Revelation 21–22. How is the city similar to the Garden of Eden? How does it differ? What does this tell us about the direction of history?

The New Jerusalem of Revelation 21–22 reminds us of the Garden of Eden in important ways. Like the Garden, a river flows through the middle of the city and on either side of the river is the tree of life (22:1–2). Yet there are important differences too. The New Jerusalem is a city made of precious jewels that will contain the glory of all the kings of the earth.

These differences show us the progress of history. God did not intend Adam to remain in the Garden forever. He was to be fruitful and multiply and bring the surrounding land under his dominion. In other words, he was to domesticate creation and turn the wilderness into a glorious city. The New Jerusalem is that city.

3. How is the Song of Solomon related to the creation of Adam and Eve in Genesis 2? See Song of Solomon 4:12–16; 5:1; 6:2.

The garden imagery used in the Song of Solomon is meant to remind us of the Garden of Eden. The romance between Solomon and the Shulammite points backward to Adam and Eve and forward to Christ, the second Adam, and His faithful love for His bride, the Church. This is why the New

Jerusalem is also described as a "bride adorned for her husband" (Rev. 21:2).

4. Hebrews 5:14 speaks of the "mature" who have their senses trained "to know good and evil." How does this verse help us understand the "tree of the knowledge of good and evil" in Genesis 2?

Hebrews 5:14 suggests that the "knowledge of good and evil" was withheld from Adam and Eve until a future time when their maturity was confirmed. Adam and Eve were not prepared for that understanding when they were first created, and God forbade them from eating from the Tree of the Knowledge of Good and Evil for their protection.

5. Consider how the story of Israel in Judges, Kings, and Ezra-Nehemiah moves through the three areas described in Genesis 2 (garden and worship, land and brother, world and unbelievers).

The story of Israel's idolatry in Judges parallels Adam's idolatry in the Garden when he listens to the voice of Satan and serves another god. Similarly, when Israel had entered the land, they fought among themselves (divided kingdom) just as Cain killed Abel in the land outside the Garden. Finally, Nehemiah rebuked Israel because they had intermarried with the ungodly nations just as the sons of God had intermarried with the daughters of men in Genesis 6.

Between Babel and Bethel:
Genesis 11–12, 17, 35

REVIEW QUESTIONS [pages 58–65]

1. Who is involved in building the tower of Babel? What are they trying to build?

The transition between Genesis 10 and 11 (10:30–11:2) indicates that the people who journeyed east were descendants of Joktan, a descendant of Noah's son Shem. A faithful line of descendents, the line of Shem, join forces with Nimrod (Gen. 10:10) to "make a name for themselves" in defiance of the Lord's command to fill the earth. By building a "tower whose top will reach into heaven," they were trying to create a sanctuary for Babylonian gods in the land of the east away from the presence of the Lord. They were trying to reestablish the "Garden" through their own efforts.

2. Explain how the story of the tower of Babel is put together. What happens in the middle of the story?

The story of the tower of Babel (Gen. 11:1–9) is structured in a chiasm, a literary structure that moves toward a center point and then back out again with the second half matching the first half in reverse order (i.e., a, b, c, D, c', b', a'). The first half of the story speaks of men's efforts to reach up into heaven to exalt their own name and to prevent themselves from being scattered over the earth. At the center point, the Lord comes down to judge their work. The second half shows the result of His judgment: the people's language is confused, they are scattered, and the work on the tower stops.

3. How is God's call to Abram connected to the story of Babel?

The genealogy of Shem, which began at the end of Genesis 10, continues after the narrative of the Tower of Babel (11:10ff). The genealogy ends with Abram (11:26). Ironically, the Lord promises to make Abram's name great and to make him the father of a great nation (12:2), which were both things the Shemites sought at Babel.

4. What are the main promises given to Abram? How are these connected with the story of Babel? How are they connected with Adam?

God promises Abram that his descendants would build the true "Babylon" ("Gate of God"). Specifically, first He promises to give Abram a "seed." Adam was given a command: "be fruitful and multiply," but Abram is given a promise: "I will make you fruitful." Adam is told to build a large household, but God promises He will build Abram's house (Gen. 17:2, 6). The result is that Abram's "house" will build God's house (through Solomon).

Second, God also promises to give Abram land (Gen. 12:7; 15:13–14, 16, 18). Abram travels west from Ur to arrive at the "promised" land, showing that the land will be a new Eden where the Lord will dwell with His people.

5. What is circumcision? What does it mean?

Circumcision is the sign of God's covenant with Abram. The action of "cutting" Abram's flesh symbolizes the cutting off of the old to receive the new. In circumcision the Old Abram dies and Abraham is raised to be the father of the "child of promise." The flesh is removed because it is powerless to realize what God has promised. Circumcision shows that Abram believes that only Yahweh can build his house and give life to Sarah's womb.

6. Explain the connections between Jacob's dream and the tower of Babel.

In his dream, Jacob sees a ladder reaching into heaven. Like the tower of Babel, whose "head" was to touch heaven, the ladder's "head" extends into heaven (28:12). However, the chief difference is that the ladder is built by God, not by Jacob. The location of the Shemites in Genesis 11:2 is undisclosed ("there"), and initially the "place" where Jacob dreams is undisclosed as well. But the "place" is transformed into a "holy place" by Yahweh's presence.

7. What does Jacob call the place where he sees the dream? Why is this important?

Jacob calls the place the "gate of Heaven," which reminds us of the Babylonian "gate of God." Later, he changes the name to Bethel, which means "the house of God." "Bethel" reveals God's answer to Babel: "He will build a way to connect heaven and earth; He will build it in the land; and he will build it though Jacob's seed."

8. What happens while Jacob is in Haran working for Laban?

Even though Laban oppresses Jacob and tries to get the better of him, the Lord keeps the promise He gave at Bethel and blesses Jacob. When Jacob returns to Bethel from exile, he has become two large companies.

9. Explain how the three patriarchs are related to the three sins early in the book of Genesis.

The early chapters of Genesis detail three major sins: one in the Garden, one in the land, and one in the world. The patriarchs reverse each of these three sins: Abraham reverses Adam's sin against God in the garden by being a faithful priest who is willing to obey the word of the Lord and sacrifice his own son; Jacob reverses Cain's sin against his brother in the land by enduring troubles with his family (Esau and Laban); Joseph reverses the sin of the "sons of God" to unbelievers by showing himself a faithful "son of God" who resists the "daughters of men" (Gen. 39:7–12).

10. Why is it fitting for Joseph's story to be at the end of Genesis?

Genesis begins with God's command to Adam to "subdue and rule" the earth; the book ends with Joseph subduing the earth and ruling the empire of Egypt. Joseph is a picture of what Adam was to become.

THOUGHT QUESTIONS

1. Yahweh tells Abram that his seed will be like the stars (Gen. 15:5). In light of the three-story house, what is the Lord telling Abram?

Throughout the Old Testament, stars—which are in the upper-story of God's creation-house—symbolize rulers. When God promises Abram in Genesis 15:5 that He will make his descendants like the stars of heaven, He is promising that Abram's descendants will rule over the earth.

2. Where does Abraham go to sacrifice Isaac (Gen. 22:2)? Compare to 2 Chronicles 3:1. What is the significance of this connection?

In Genesis 22:2, Abraham goes to Mount Moriah to sacrifice his son, Isaac. Later, Solomon builds the temple, a place of sacrifice, on the same mountain. The fact that the Levites and Abraham offered "sacrifices" on the same spot gives us insight into the purpose of the sacrificial system as a whole. The animals sacrificed in the temple all point to the "coming sacrifice of the new Isaac." The temple of the Church is built on the sacrificial blood of Jesus, the new Isaac.

3. Read Genesis 25:23. In light of what the Lord says here, evaluate Isaac's preference for Esau. See also 25:34; 26:34–35.

Isaac favored Esau and gave him the blessing of the first born, making Esau the heir to his wealth, power, and authority, even though the Lord had told him that Esau would serve Jacob. His preference indicates that he preferred the tasty game that Esau brought him over obedience to the Lord's word. Isaac rebelled against God in showing favor to Esau.

4. Judah becomes one of the most prominent sons of Jacob. Yet, he is not the firstborn but the fourth son of Leah. Why? Look at Genesis 34 and 35:22.

Reuben, Simeon, and Levi, the eldest of Jacob's sons, were all denied the firstborn's birthright because of their sin. Judah, though he is the fourth born, receives what was theirs. Jacob's blessing of his sons appears in Genesis 49:10.

5. Genesis 38 is a story about Judah, yet it comes in the middle of the section of Genesis that is dealing with Joseph. Why? Look at Genesis 39:7–18 and 44:14–34.

The story of Judah and Tamar in Genesis 38 provides a vivid contrast to Joseph's faithful dealings with Potiphar's wife in Genesis 39. Joseph is unwilling to defile himself with the "daughters of men." The account of events about Joseph is necessary to understand Judah's story. In Genesis 49, Jacob blesses Joseph, but gives Judah the scepter to Judah and calls him a ruler. Most importantly, the seed passes through the line of Judah.

CHAPTER 2

OUT OF EGYPT HAVE I CALLED MY SON

A King Who Knows Not Joseph: *Exodus 1–2*
The Marriage Supper of Yaweh: *Exodus 20–24*

REVIEW QUESTIONS [pages 71–81]

1. What is Laban looking for in Genesis 31?

Laban is looking for his household gods.

2. What does the story of Laban's gods teach us?

The story teaches us that Laban's household gods are no gods at all. In Genesis 31, Rachel is sitting on Laban's gods, preventing them from "escape." Moreover, since Rachel is sitting on them during the time of her monthly period, Laban's gods have also become unclean (Lev. 15:19–24). Unclean gods make the people who worship them unclean as well. All of this shows that idols have no power to stand against the Lord.

3. Explain how the story in Genesis 31 is like the story in Exodus.

Like the Israelites in Exodus, Jacob leaves the land to go to live with his uncle Laban, is oppressed by his uncle, and then returns to the land with more wealth than he had before. Jacob's story is an exodus story.

4. How is Abram's exodus like the exodus of Israel?

Like Jacob's sons, Abram went to Egypt to find food. While there his wife is taken "captive" into Pharaoh's household and God visits the Egyptians with "plagues." Finally, Abram leaves Egypt with great wealth.

5. Explain the connections between the beginning and end of Exodus.

At the beginning of the book of Exodus, the Israelites are enslaved to a wicked king who forces them to build his "house" and tells Moses that Israel belongs to him. By the end of the book, the Lord takes His throne as King of Israel (Exod. 40:34–38) in the Tabernacle that Israel built, showing that Israel belongs to Him.

6. Explain the "wedding ceremony" of Yahweh and Israel at Sinai.

God's covenant with Israel at Mount Sinai is like a wedding ceremony. The "marriage" is officiated by Moses who brings the Lord's word down to the people. Yahweh, the bridegroom, reminds Israel of His past faithfulness (Exod. 20:1–2) and promises that He will provide for Israel, His bride, and bestow on her good gifts if she will obey and honor Him (Exod. 20–23). Israel responds to Yahweh by promising to honor Him and obey all of His commandments (Exod. 24:3). The ceremony ends with a wedding feast in the Lord's presence (Exod. 24:9–11). Yahweh then moves in with His bride, and the rest of Exodus is concerned with building Yahweh's house (Exod. 25–40).

7. How are the laws of Exodus based on God's rescue of His people?

In Exodus 20–23, God tells Israel how to live as His servants. Many of the commands are rooted in the Exodus. The Lord tells Israel that they are to live according to His commandments *because* they were once slaves in the land of Egypt. Now that the Lord has rescued them from bondage, they should live like a saved people. Specifically, because Israel has been delivered from slavery, they should also deliver others from slavery (Exod. 21:1–11). Israel has also been given Sabbath rest (from the oppression of Egypt), and they should give that rest to others (Exod. 20:8–11; Deut. 5:12–15).

8. How is the tabernacle related to the tower of Babel?

At the beginning of Exodus, Israel is busy building Pharaoh's kingdom. At the end of the book, Israel is building a tabernacle for Yahweh. This is a fulfillment of God's promise to Abram in Genesis 12. Abram was God's answer to the Tower of Babel. Now, at the end of Exodus, God has built Israel into a numerous people, and they are ready to build a house for Yahweh's name.

THOUGHT QUESTIONS

1. The Hebrew midwives deceive Pharaoh in order to protect the Hebrew children (Exod. 1:15–22). Is this right? Does God punish them for doing this? Compare Genesis 12:11–13.

Exodus 1:15–22 specifically says that the Hebrew midwives deceived Pharaoh because they "feared the Lord." It also notes that "God was good to the midwives and the people multiplied and became very mighty." Similarly, in Genesis 12:11–13 Abram tells his wife to deceive the Egyptians about her true relation to Abram. The resulting judgment on Egypt and blessing on Abram's household (Gen. 13:1–2) show that Abram found favor with the Lord.

2. When Yahweh strikes Egypt with gnats, the magicians of Egypt recognize that the "finger of God" is at work (Exod. 8:19). Compare Luke 11:20. What does this connection say about Jesus? What does it say about the Jews who oppose Jesus?

When Jesus casts out "demons by the finger of God," He is showing that another Exodus is about to happen. This time, however, Israel is being held "captive" by her religious leaders (who reject the Jesus, the new Moses), and Jesus is indicating that the Jews will be judged just like Pharaoh and his armies and their hearts will grow cold.

3. When Israel crosses the sea, the waters are divided and dry land appears (Exod. 14:22). How is this connected to Genesis 1:9–13?

The imagery of the divided water and the dry land remind us that Israel's exodus is the beginning of a new creation.

4. What is the punishment for theft (Exod. 22:4)? How does this illustrate the principle of "eye for eye, tooth for tooth" (Exod. 21:23–25)?

According to Exodus 22:4, if a man steals an animal and it is found alive in his possession, he must repay double (the original animal plus one from his own flock). This means that he must give from his own possessions to make up for the evil he intended against his neighbor. In the end, he loses the exact amount he hoped to gain ("an eye for an eye").

5. Many Christians believe that the Old Testament law was harsh compared to Jesus' emphasis on loving your enemies. Look at Exodus 23:4–9. Was Jesus teaching anything new?

When Jesus says that we should "love our enemies" (Mt. 5:43–48), He is not teaching a new and gentler law. He is rather returning to true intent of the law, which, as Exodus 23:4–9 shows, has always required God's people to love their enemies.

The House of the Lord: *Exodus 25–40*

REVIEW QUESTIONS [pages 82–86]

1. What is the tabernacle?

The tabernacle is the house that Israel built for Yahweh at Sinai. It was made of canvas and wood (Exod. 26:15ff) and was positioned with its door to the East (Num. 1:53; 3:23, 29, 35, 38–39).

2. What are the three zones of the tabernacle?

Inside the Tabernacle are two rooms: the larger area is called the Holy Place while inner room is called the Most Holy Place or "Holy of Holies." Outside of these is a third area called the courtyard. These three zones are governed by a different set of rules. Laymen can enter the courtyard, but only priests can enter the Holy Place, and only the High Priest can enter the Most Holy Place once a year on the Day of Atonement (Lev. 16:1).

3. What is in each of the three "rooms" of the tabernacle?

Each "room" of the tabernacle contains furniture. In the courtyard is a bronze altar that is used for animal offerings. The courtyard also contains the bronze laver, set between the altar and the tent, in which the priests wash before entering the Holy Place (Exod. 30:17–21). In the Holy Place, on the north side, is a wooden table overlaid with gold (Exod. 25:23–30) that holds twelve loaves of shewbread which are replaced each Sabbath day (Lev. 24:5–9). To the South is a lampstand of gold in the form of an almond tree (Exod. 25:31–40). On the West side, in front of the veil that separates the Holy Place from the Most Holy Place, is the golden altar of incense (Exod. 30:1–10). The Most Holy Place contains the ark of the covenant (Exod. 25:10–22).

4. How is the tabernacle like a house? Whose house is it?

The tabernacle has rooms and furniture like a house. In the court there is an altar (stove) for cooking food, which is also called the Lord's "table" (Ezek. 44:16). In the Holy Place there is a lamp, an altar for incense, and a table with bread. The Most Holy Place is Yahweh's throne room. In it is the ark, God's footstool, which contains the two tablets of the Ten Commandments; the cherubim above form the Lord's throne.

5. What is a "sanctuary"? What makes the tabernacle a "sanctuary"?

The word "sanctuary" means holy place. Throughout the Bible, places become holy when the Lord visits them in His glory (Exod. 3). In Exodus 29:43–44, Yahweh descends on the Tabernacle in a glory-cloud and makes it His. Following this, the Lord institutes rules that govern how His holy house is to be handled.

6. How is the tabernacle like Sinai?

Mt. Sinai and the tabernacle are structured similarly; both contain three "zones." The people of Israel may approach the base of Sinai but are not allowed to touch it (Exod. 19:20–25). The elders of Israel are allowed to go halfway up the mountain, but no higher (Exod. 24:1–8). Only Moses, as Israel's representative, is permitted to meet with the Lord at the top of the mountain. In the same way, the people are allowed to enter the courtyard of the Tabernacle, but are not to touch the altar. The priests work in the Holy Place, but only the High Priest is allowed to enter the Most Holy Place once a year.

7. How is the tabernacle like the "house" of Israel? How does this help explain the sacrifices?

Like the Tabernacle, Israel herself is divided into three groups. Most of the people are not priests while all of Aaron's sons are priests; however, of all Aaron's sons, only one is the High Priest. Since the house of God represents the house of Israel, the priests are only required to sprinkle blood on various parts of the Tabernacle and not on the people. Putting blood on the Tabernacle is like putting it on the people.

8. How is the tabernacle similar to the original creation?

The creation is structured in three stories: highest heaven (the throne of God), the firmament (part of the heavens), the land (Israel), and the sea (the nations). Each of these correspond to an area of the Tabernacle. The Most Holy Place is the throne of God, the Holy Place is linked to the firmament (Ps. 150:1), and the courtyard is where the people of Israel gather.

9. In what ways is the tabernacle like the Garden of Eden?

Like the Garden, the entrance to the Tabernacle is on the East, and there are Cherubim on the veil separating the Most Holy Place from the Holy Place to guard the entrance to God's throne (Exod. 26:31–37). The people of Israel, like Adam, are prohibited from approaching God's dwelling place.

THOUGHT QUESTIONS

1. Notice how the materials of the tabernacle furniture change as you move from the courtyard to the Most Holy Place. What metals are used? Why?

The furniture in the courtyard is made of bronze while the furniture in the Holy Place is overlaid with gold or made with pure gold, and in the Most Holy Place the piece is covered inside and out with gold. The closer things get to the presence of the Lord the more glorious they are.

2. Compare the materials of the tabernacle curtains and veils (Exod. 26:31–37) with the materials of the garments of the High Priest (Exod. 28:5–6). What does this tell you about the High Priest? See John 1:14.

The garments of the High Priest are made from the same material as the curtains and veils of the Tabernacle. This likeness symbolizes the High Priest's role as a mediator; once a year he stands between Yahweh and Israel to make atonement for their sins. Since Jesus has come, there is no longer a tabernacle or temple on earth. This means God is no longer keeping us away from Him.

3. The Spirit of God is mentioned only a few times in the Pentateuch. Two of the times are Genesis 1:2 and Exodus 31:3. Are these passages connected? How?

In Genesis 1:2 the Spirit hovers over the unformed substance of the earth before it is fashioned into God's creation-house. In Exodus 31:3 the Spirit fills the craftsmen who are working on the Tabernacle and enables them to build God's new house. The Tabernacle is a new creation.

4. Israel's sin with the golden calf is recorded in Exodus 32, in the middle of the description of the tabernacle. What does this suggest about the golden calf?

The tabernacle was a place where God chose to meet His people. He built it because He knew that the Israelites needed to see visual proof of His presence. When Moses went up to Mount Sinai, the Israelites were without a leader. Left to their own devices, they mimicked the Egyptians and fashioned a visual god. They created the golden calf to represent their missing god. God provided a tabernacle not only so the people could sense His presence, but so their leaders would not have to disappear into the mountains.

5. Why does Moses break the tablets of the law when he sees Israel worshiping the golden calf (Exod. 32:15–20)?

Moses was angry and the text says, "his anger burned hot." He broke the tablets containing God's covenant with Israel because Israel had broken their covenant with God by worshiping the golden calf.

Bread of God: *Leviticus 1–7*
Servants of the Lord's House:
Exodus 28–29, Leviticus 8–9

REVIEW QUESTIONS [pages 87–97]

1. What is a *qorban*? How does an offering renew fellowship between God and the worshiper?

The word *qorban* means "gift" or "something brought near" (Lev. 1:2; 2:1; 3:1–2; 4:23; 5:11; 7:38). In Israel exchanging gifts is a way of making a covenant between people (just as people exchange rings at a wedding). At Sinai, Yahweh "married" Israel and promised to give her good gifts if she was faithful to Him. Gifts (*qorban*) are also the way individuals draw near to God.

In the Old Testament, because of the sin of Adam, Israel is kept away from God and may not fully enter into His presence. In this act of gift-giving, the offering stands in place of the worshiper as his representative and shows that he is really offering himself to God. This is the sacrifice that Yahweh desires (1 Sam. 15:22–23). Thus, when a faithful Israelite brings an animal to the Lord, he is renewing fellowship and is promising to serve and obey Yahweh in faithfulness.

2. In what sense are the animal offerings "bread for God"?

When a worshiper presents an offering, he is bringing a meal to God (Lev. 3:11, 16; 21:6; Num. 28:2). Though God doesn't need to eat to live, He "eats" Israel's sacrifices as a sign of His friendship. He "eats," continuing the wedding feast that began on Sinai. Also, since the flesh of animals represents people, the offerings show that really God desires the "flesh" of His people, which means people who love and obey Him.

3. What are the five basic steps of the animal offerings?

The five basic steps of the animal offerings are:
1. The worshiper lays his hands on the animal's head, setting it apart and demonstrating that the animal is acting as his substitute.
2. The worshiper slaughters the animal in place of himself.
3. The priest presents (sprinkles) the blood of the animal in the tabernacle, showing that the animal died in place of the worshiper. We see the same principle at Passover (Exod. 12:1–12).
4. The flesh of the animal is burned on the bronze altar in the courtyard of the tabernacle and is accepted as a sweet-smelling savor by the Lord.
5. Finally, the rite of offering ends with a fellowship meal which renews the covenant and shows that the worshiper and God are friends.

4. What is the meaning of laying hands on the animal's head?

Laying hands on something is a way of setting it apart for a particular job or office (Num. 27:18ff; Deut. 34:9; Acts 6:6). In this case the animal is set apart to be the worshiper's representative or substitute. When the animal is "accepted" in the worshiper's place, the worshiper is also accepted before God.

5. Why does the priest put the blood on the tabernacle furniture after the animal has died?

The priest sprinkles the blood of the offering on the tabernacle furniture in order to show that death has taken place. Before the worshiper, who is a sinner, can draw near to God, he must show that something or someone has died in his place.

6. What is the meaning of burning the animal?

The word for "burning" the animal literally means "to turn into smoke." Passing though the fire, the animal is purified, transformed, glorified, and rises to become part of the cloud of God's presence over the altar. The fire of the Lord "eats" the offering. It is a sign that the Lord accepts the offering as a substitute for the worshiper.

7. How is the meal after an offering connected with the covenant?

After the sacrifice the worshiper and the priest eat a fellowship meal—the meat of the animal that was offered—in the Lord's presence. Yahweh invites the worshiper to eat in His presence as a sign of friendship. It is also a sign that the covenant has been reaffirmed and that there is peace between the worshiper and Yahweh.

8. How is the "ascension offering" different from the other offerings? The peace offering? The purification offering?

The ascension offering (Lev. 1) is the only offering that is entirely (minus the skin, which goes to the priests) offered up in smoke on the altar. The peace offering (Lev. 3) is the only offering that the worshiper is allowed to eat. The peace offering is divided into four shares and then Yahweh, the priests, and the worshiper all eat a fellowship meal together. The purification or sin offering (Lev. 4) highlights the sprinkling of blood and involves different sprinkling rituals depending on the one bringing the offering.

9. What is the difference between the purification offering and the reparation offering?

The purification offering cleanses an unclean person of his uncleanness or a sinner from his sin. The reparation offering turns a holy person back to the status of a commoner. If a person touches something that is holy he becomes holy, but if a person is not prepared to be holy, becoming consecrated is dangerous. A reparation (guilt) offering "de-sanctifies" an individual, safely returning him to a common status.

10. What is a priest? What does a priest do?

A priest is a "household servant" of the Lord. Only priests are allowed to enter the sanctuary, and only the High Priest can enter the Most Holy Place once a year on the Day of

Atonement. Priests offer incense and trim the wicks of the lamps morning and evening (Exod. 30:7–8; Lev. 24:1–4), and they replace the showbread on the golden table every Sabbath (Lev. 24:5–9).

In the courtyard, the priests offer sacrifices morning and night and on feast days (Num. 28–29), help the Israelites offer offerings, guard the tabernacle (Num. 3:8, 38), and receive firstfruits, tithes, and votive offerings (Lev. 27; Num. 18). They also decide when a person is clean or unclean and do rites of cleansing (Lev. 12–15). In return for their service, the priests receive tithes and portions of the sacrifices (Lev. 7–8; Num. 18).

Priest also have duties that are more like the duties of Christian pastors. They ask God questions (Exod. 28:30; Num. 27:21). Priests teach the law (Deut. 33:10; Lev. 10:8–11; cf. Jer. 18:18; Hosea 4:4–6; Mal. 2:1–9), and in certain cases, they serve as judges (Deut. 17:9).

THOUGHT QUESTIONS

1. Leviticus 2:2 says that a priest puts a "memorial" of the grain offering on the altar. Who receives this memorial portion? Jesus uses a similar word when instituting the Lord's Supper, saying that the Supper is His "memorial." In light of Leviticus 2:2, who is "receiving" the memorial in the Supper?

In Leviticus 2:2, the priest offers the memorial portion of the grain offering on the altar to Yahweh. In the same way, Jesus' use of the same word while instituting the Lord's Supper shows us that the Supper is a memorial—a "reminder"—to the Father of what Jesus has accomplished in His death and resurrection.

2. In Leviticus 6:1–5, a man who steals something has to pay back what he stole and add a fifth of the value. In Exodus 22:4, he has to pay back twice as much as he stole. Why the difference?

In Leviticus 6:1–5, one who steals feels remorse, repents, and confesses his sin and returns the items. The person in Exodus

22:4 is caught with the stolen goods in his possession. This shows that there is a built-in incentive in the law for a person to give up before he gets caught. The penalty is lowered for the one who repents.

3. What is done with the "sin offering" on the Day of Atonement (Lev. 16:11–22)? How is this different from other sin offerings?

On the Day of Atonement, the High Priest enters the Most Holy Place and sprinkles the blood of a bull (for his sins) and a goat (for the sins of the people) on and to the side of the mercy seat. He also takes some of the blood from the bull and goat and atones for the altar of ascension by smearing blood on its horns. Finally, the High Priest takes a live goat and, placing his hands on its head, transfers all of Israel's sin to it and sends it out into the wilderness. All of this is done once a year to atone for the sins of the whole nation.

4. What kinds of defects disqualify a descendant of Aaron from serving as priest (Lev. 21:16–24)? Compare Leviticus 22:17–25. What do these passages suggest about what it means to be a priest?

Any kind of physical defect or blemish prevents a descendant of Aaron from being a priest. The requirements suggest that a priest must be perfect, like the animal he offers, because he stands in the presence of the Lord who is holy. These requirements ultimately point to Jesus, who was both the perfect offering for the sins of His people and the perfect High Priest who lives always to make intercession for us (Heb. 9–10).

5. How many bulls are offered as burnt offerings during the course of the Feast of Booths (Num. 29:12–38)? What does this tell us about the meaning of the Feast of Booths?

The total number of bulls offered at the Feast of Booths is significant. The total number offered is seventy, the number of the Gentile nations in Genesis 10. This means that the Feast of the Booths, which is a feast celebrating the ingathering of the harvest, pictures the "ingathering" of the Gentiles into the people of God.

CHAPTER 3

FROM SINAI TO SHILOH

Rebellion in the Wilderness: *Numbers 1–7, 13–14*

REVIEW QUESTIONS [pages 101–105]

1. What are the first ten chapters of Numbers about? Why is this important?

The first ten chapters emphasize how God is organizing His people in the wilderness. Every tribe is given a place as the house of Israel is camped around the house of their King. This is important because it shows how God is making the world new and is preparing His people to be a nation of new of Adams and Eves. The presence of the glory-cloud at the center of the camp reminds us of the original creation and God's presence and friendship with Adam and Eve.

2. Why are the numbers in Numbers important?

In the book of Numbers, the fighting men of Israel are "numbered" at the beginning and then again at its end (Num. 1, 26). The result of the numberings shows how God has been faithful to His promise to make Abraham's seed as numerous as the sand on the seashore.

3. What is the title for Numbers in the Hebrew Bible?

The Hebrew name for Numbers means "in the wilderness."

4. How does Israel behave in the wilderness? How does God punish them?

In the Bible, the wilderness is a place of testing, and Israel reveals her unbelief by continually disobeying the word of the Lord. Often, the Lord responds to Israel's sin by giving them what they want. Israel wants to die in the wilderness, and the Lord lets them.

5. What happens at Kadesh? Why is this such a serious sin?

At Kadesh, Moses sends twelve spies to investigate the land. When they return, all but Joshua and Caleb respond in unbelief and claim that the people who live there are too strong for them. This unbelief constitutes the ultimate act of rebellion toward all of the Lord's promises.

6. What does "Kadesh" mean? Why is this significant?

Kadesh means "holy place." An earlier name for Kadesh also means "well of judgment." Kadesh is a well-watered place in the wilderness, a small picture of the land God had promised Israel. But instead of entering in faith, Israel sins in the "garden-sanctuary" and fails to enter the new Eden-land.

7. Explain the connections between Abram's war and the events at Kadesh.

In Genesis 13–14, Abram had conquered the very land the spies visited with 318 fighting men while Israel's 600,000 fighting men refuse to fight out of fear. Even though they are children of Abram, Israel does not have the faith of their father.

8. Explain how God's punishment of the ten spies fits the crime.

The ten spies accuse the land of murder (Num. 13:32), and they are killed as false witnesses against the land (Num. 14:36–37; cf. Deut. 19:16–19). The people want to die in the wilderness (Num. 14:2), and God lets them. Since the people refuse to enter the Eden-land, God forbids them from entering. Israel gets what she wants, but when she receives it, she doesn't want it anymore.

9. How is the book of Numbers a story of the "death and resurrection" of Israel?

Because Israel rebels against the Lord at Kadesh, the old generation is condemned to die in the wilderness. But by the end of Numbers, a new generation has taken their place. Old Israel has died, but a new Israel has risen to new life.

10. What happens after the death of Aaron? Why is this important?

Aaron's death marks the end of the older generation. After his death, Israel wins their first victory over the Canaanites (21:1–3, 21–35). His death as high priest symbolizes the end of Israel's wandering in the "city of refuge" (i.e., the wilderness, see Num. 35:22–34). When Aaron dies, Israel is allowed to enter the Promised Land.

THOUGHT QUESTIONS

1. Numbers 5:1–4 says that certain groups of people have to be removed from the camp. Who are they? Why are they removed? What does this say about the camp?

Numbers 5:1–4 requires that everyone who is a leper, who has a discharge, or who is unclean because of a dead person be sent outside the camp so they don't defile the place where the Lord lives. This underscores the Lord's holiness and its effect on the entire camp of Israel—He makes it clean by dwelling there, and anything that defiles the camp must be removed.

2. What is the test for an adulterous woman in Numbers 5:11–31? How does this relate to Moses' actions in Exodus 32:19–20?

The woman is called to stand before the Lord and she is put under oath. She is required to drink bitter water. If she lied under oath, the Lord would cause her people to curse and denounce her when her thigh wastes away and her abdomen swells. By grinding up the Golden Calf and making Israel drink it, Moses is asking the Lord to judge His people who have played the harlot and are guilty of unfaithfulness.

3. The Hebrew word for "almond" sounds a lot like the Hebrew word for "watcher." How does this help us understand Aaron's budding rod in Numbers 17?

Part of Aaron's duty is to be a guardian and "watcher" over Israel. The fact that his rod blossoms when it is put before the Lord indicates that his labor of "watching" will bear fruit.

4. Who is Balaam (Num. 22:5–14)? Why is it funny that his donkey sees the angel of the Lord before he does?

Balaam is a "seer." Part of the irony of this situation is that the "seer" can't see what is right in front of him. His donkey is a better "seer" than he is.

5. Why does Moses get angry at the tribes of Reuben and Gad (Num. 32:1–27)?

Moses is angry at the tribes of Reuben and Gad because they want to settle in the land of the Transjordan. This appears to be a replay of the rebellion at Kadesh (Num. 13–14), but Reuben and Gad assure Moses they will cross over the Jordan and help the other tribes subdue the land before they return.

War and Rest: *Deuteronomy 12; Joshua 1–12*

REVIEW QUESTIONS [pages 106–112]

1. What is in the book of Deuteronomy?

Deuteronomy is a collection of sermons Moses preaches to Israel while they are still in Moab before they enter the Promised Land. Since this generation is a new Israel, God renews His covenant (made at Sinai) with them. Moses reminds Israel of the things they must do when they enter the land so that they may dwell in it in peace.

2. According to Deuteronomy 12, what is Israel's mission?

According to Deuteronomy 12, Israel is to utterly destroy all the places where "the nations whom you shall dispossess serve their gods, on the high mountains and on the hills and under every green tree. And you shall tear down their altars and smash their sacred pillars and burn their Asherim with fire, and you shall cut down the engraved images of their gods, and you shall obliterate their name from that place" (Deut. 12:2–3).

3. What is Israel supposed to remember? Why?

One of the most significant words in Deuteronomy is "remember." At Kadesh, the old Israel forgot what the Lord had done for them and consequently, they died in the wilderness. Moses' song at the end of Deuteronomy reminds Israel of the covenant God made with them so that their conquest of the land will be successful.

4. How is Joshua like Moses? Why does the book of Joshua show these similarities?

The book of Joshua presents Joshua as a new Moses. Joshua leads Israel across the Jordan as Moses led Israel though the Red Sea. Once they enter the land, Joshua has the men of Israel circumcised just as Moses had to circumcise his son when he reentered Egypt after sojourning in Midian. Joshua reinstates the Passover, which was instituted by Moses to commemorate Israel's deliverance from Egypt. Joshua meets the angel of the Lord and has to remove his shoes just like Moses before the burning bush. Joshua also sends spies into the land as did Moses. All of these similarities are meant to show us that God has appointed a new Moses to lead a "new" Israel.

5. Give a summary of the conquest.

There are three main stages of the conquest. First, Israel conquers Jericho and heads north to defeat Ai. This gives them control of the central territory. After renewing the covenant on the mountains of Gerazim and Ebal (Josh. 8:30–35), the conquest is divided into two main campaigns. In the South, Joshua saves the city of Gibeon from the king of Jerusalem. Then in the North, Israel is attacked by the kings of the North, led by Jabin, king of Hazor, at the waters of Merom. Joshua defeats these kings and Hazor is offered as a "whole burnt offering" to the Lord.

6. What is unusual about Israel's strategy at Jericho? What kind of warfare is this?

Joshua's strategy at Jericho focuses on the priests instead of the army. This plan shows us that Israel's warfare, unlike the warfare of other ancient peoples, is an act of worship. When Israel worships God, He gives them victory.

7. What happened at the first battle of Ai? What did Israel learn from this?

Israel was defeated at the first battle of Ai because Achan had taken some of the forbidden plunder of Jericho, which was set apart to the Lord, and consequently had made Israel unholy. From this battle Israel learned that in order to have success she had to remain holy. As with Jericho, faithful worship is the key to conquest.

8. How is Joshua's movement through the land like Abraham's? Why is this important?

Like Abraham, Joshua conquers the land through faithful worship. Israel's path of conquest covers much of the same area Abraham traveled through as he divided the land by setting up altars. This again emphasizes that "once the land is consecrated to the Lord by worship, eventually the land will be conquered."

9. What is the last half of the book of Joshua about?

The last half of Joshua describes the division of the land between the tribes of Israel.

10. What happens in the middle of dividing up the land? Why is this important?

In the midst of the division, Israel sets up the tabernacle at Shiloh (Josh. 18:1). This makes the land a holy land, a land where Yahweh has set up His royal residence. Joshua also establishes forty-eight Levitical cities, in obedience to Moses, where the Law is to be studied and taught. Despite the success of the conquest, Canaanite shrines still remained and if Israel was to remain the land she had been given, she would need to worship faithfully at Shiloh and listen to the Law of God taught throughout the land.

THOUGHT QUESTIONS

1. What does Rahab have to put in her window in order to save her house from destruction (Josh. 2:17–18)? Why? Compare Exodus 12:7, 13.

Rahab was commanded to put a scarlet cord in her window to save her house from destruction. It was a symbol of the blood that Israel placed on their houses at Passover so that the judgment visited upon the Egyptians would pass them by. The scarlet cord identifies Rahab with God's people, and the judgment of Jericho passes her by.

2. What effect does Israel's crossing of the Jordan have on the Canaanites (Josh. 5:1)? Explain the connection of this verse with Exodus 15:14–16. Compare Genesis 35.

When Israel crosses the Jordan, the Canaanites tremble in fear as they previously feared Moses and no longer have the courage to face the Israelites. This second "passing through the waters" is important because Israel left Egypt by passing through the Red Sea, and here they enter the land by passing through the Jordan. In a sense, these are different parts of the same "crossing." The Jordan crossing is a fulfillment of the promise in Exodus 15. This also reminds us of the fear that fell upon the inhabitants of the land when Jacob journeyed to Bethel (Gen. 35:5).

3. In Joshua 9, Joshua agrees to make peace with the Gibeonites. Discuss how this passage serves as background for what happens in 2 Samuel 21.

In 2 Samuel 21 there is a famine in the land of Israel because Saul has broken the covenant Joshua made with the Gibeonites by putting them to death. David makes restitution by giving seven men from Saul's family into the hands of the Gibeonites to be hanged. David then takes the bones of Saul, Jonathan, and the seven who have been hanged and buries them in the grave of Kish, Saul's father. His actions bring an end to the famine.

4. What are cities of refuge used for (Josh. 20:1–9)?

The cities of refuge are designed to remove blood guiltiness from the land. If a man accidentally kills his neighbor, he can flee to one of the cities of refuge where he will be protected from the blood avenger. He has to remain in the city until the death of the high priest, and then he can return in peace to his home.

5. Why does Joshua get angry with the tribes of Reuben and Gad (Josh. 22)?

After Joshua dismisses the tribes of Reuben and Gad to return to their inheritance on the other side of the Jordan, Reuben and Gad build an altar over against the land of Canaan, in the borders of Jordan. The other tribes see this action as a rebellious rejection of Shiloh and a sign of division. However, Gad and Reuben insist that the altar is not for worship, but is meant to be a sign that they have an inheritance among the sons of Israel even though they are on the other side of the Jordan. This explanation satisfies Joshua and the tribes and the altar becomes a "witness" between Gad and Reuben and the rest of Israel.

No King in Israel: *Judges 8–9, 17–21*

REVIEW QUESTIONS [pages 113–118]

1. Why are the tribes of Israel unable to conquer the Canaanites?

The tribes are unable to conquer the Canaanites because they failed in their duty to destroy the altars and shrines as the Lord commanded them and even joined in Canaanite worship. Because they failed in worship, they failed in conquest.

2. Explain the "cycle" of the book of Judges from Judges 2.

In Judges 2:6–19 we find a summary of the whole book. After Joshua dies, a generation arises in Israel that does not know the Lord. Because the Israelites do not "remember" the Lord or what He had done for them, they begin to worship other gods, the gods of the nations. So God gives them their desire and shows them what it is like to be a Canaanite. He returns them to the slavery of Egypt by giving their enemies victory over them. When Israel cries out for deliverance, the Lord raises up a judge to deliver her, but after the death of the judge Israel turns back to the gods of the Canaanites and the cycle starts over again.

3. What is the sentence repeated three times at the end of Judges? What does it mean?

"There was no king in Israel; every man did what was right in his own eyes" (17:6; 18:1; 19:1). It means that Israel was ignoring her King enthroned at Shiloh and consequently was pursuing any form of worship that seemed right to her.

4. How is the book of Judges arranged? What story is at the center of the book?

The book of Judges tells about seven major judges, with Gideon at the center:

1. Othniel (3:7–11)
2. Ehud (3:12–30)
3. Deborah and Barak (4:1–5:31)
4. Gideon (6:1–8:32)
5. Abimelech (8:33–9:57)
6. Jephthah (10:6–12:7)
7. Samson (13:1–16:31)

5. What does the sign of the fleece mean? What does this say about Gideon's effect on Israel?

Gideon, a great hero of faith, wants a sign that the Lord has chosen him to deliver Israel. The sign of the fleece is showing Gideon that the Lord will deliver Israel through him. The fleece represents Gideon himself. The first sign tells Gideon that he is the dew-drenched fleece, the lamb of God filled by the Spirit. The second sign indicates that through his work as judge, the Spirit is poured out on the dry ground of Israel.

6. What happens when the Israelites want Gideon to be king? What does he do right after that?

When Israel offers to make him king, Gideon rightly refuses to accept. However, following his refusal, Gideon asks for contributions of gold (in a way that reminds us of Aaron), which he fashions into a golden ephod that leads Israel astray (Judg. 8:27). Gideon began his career known as "Jerubbaal" because he attacked idolatry; he ends his career by leading Israel into idolatry. Gideon also multiplies wives (8:30). All of this betrays the fact that even though Gideon refuses the kingdom, he is acting like an unfaithful king.

7. Who is Abimelech? What does his name mean? How does he die?

Abimelech is Gideon's son. His name means "my father is king," which further reveals Gideon's kingly intentions. Sadly, Abimelech doesn't care if Yahweh is king and sets himself to become the king his father refused to be. He is the first king of Israel. Abimelech's life is a warning to Israel that a king is not an automatic blessing. Abimelech is a serpent whose life ends with his head being crushed by a stone (Judg. 9:53).

8. What is the story of Micah about?

The story of Micah reveals how deeply the Levites had fallen into idolatry. Micah hires a Levite to work in his idolatrous shrine. Rather than serving Yahweh, the priesthood has become servants of the highest bidder. Instead of having their "hands filled" (which is the meaning of the phrase "to ordain a priest") by the Lord, the Levites have their hands full of cash and are willing to work for any idol if the price is right.

THOUGHT QUESTIONS

1. How does Sisera die (Judg. 4:17–22)? Why is this significant?

Jael "crushes" Sisera's head by driving a tent peg through his temple. This reminds us of God's promise in Genesis 3:15 that the seed of the woman will crush the serpent's head.

2. Jael is said to be "most blessed of women in the tent" (Judg. 5:24). Compare Luke 1:42. Explain the connection between the two passages.

Jael and Mary are both called "most blessed of women." Jael's victory over Sisera foreshadows Mary's declaration in the Magnificat: "He has brought rulers from their thrones, and has exalted those who were humble" (Lk. 1:52). Like Jael, Mary's son will crush the head of His enemy in fulfillment of Genesis 3:15.

3. Is Samson in sin when he finds a woman among the Philistines (Judg. 14:1)? Notice the context with 13:24–25 and see 14:4.

The problem with seeing Samson's action as a sin is that it is immediately preceded by the phrase "And the Spirit of the Lord began to stir in him" (Judg. 13:25). According to the text, Samson pursues a Philistine woman *as a result* of being moved by the Spirit. His parents were not aware that the

LORD had led him to the woman as an occasion to confront the Philistines (14:4).

4. What does the behavior of the men of Gibeah remind us of (Judg. 19:10–26)? What does this say about the condition of Israel?

The behavior of the men of Gibeah reminds of the men who gathered at Lot's door in Sodom (Gen. 19:1–11). Israel has become like the cities of Sodom and Gomorrah, which the Lord destroyed because of their wickedness.

5. Look at Judges 20:28 and answer this question: During which part of the period of the judges did these events in Gibeah take place? Why is this story placed here in Judges?

The fact that Phinehas, Aaron's son, is the high priest indicates the events of the story occur much earlier than their place in Judges would imply. The reason for this reorganization must be thematic. The author is emphasizing the theme that there is no king in Israel. To illustrate this theme, he tells stories, like Phineas's, about the Levites' failures. These failures highlight the reason there is no king in Israel: the nation has fallen into idolatrous worship, and it is because the Levites have failed to acknowledge the Lord as king.

Mercy for Widows: *Ruth*

REVIEW QUESTIONS [pages 119–122]

1. How is Ruth a story for all Israel?

During the time of the Judges, when Israel is often in deep unfaithfulness, Ruth serves as a picture of God's faithfulness in the midst of Israel's rebellion. The story of Ruth shows that God will restore all that Israel lacks, focusing on His provision of food, husbands, and sons for widows, Naomi and Ruth. Naomi is a picture of Israel, and the Lord's mercy to Naomi is a promise of mercy to His people. Israel is God's bride, but Israel has not been paying attention to her Husband. She has been looking for other husbands. So, the Lord has left Israel a widow. The message of Ruth is a message of hope for widowed Israel.

2. What kind of story do we have in Ruth 1? What's odd about it?

Ruth 1 is an exodus story. Elimelech and Naomi leave the land, and Naomi returns with Ruth. But instead of prospering outside the land as Jacob did, Naomi loses her husband and sons. Naomi goes out full and comes back empty (1:21). The rest of the book completes this strange exodus as Naomi and Ruth find rest in the land.

3. What does Naomi "lack" at the beginning of the book? How is this reversed at the end?

Naomi lacks food, and her husband and sons are dead. At the book's end God miraculously provides food, a husband, and through the redeemer Obed (4:14), a "son" for Naomi.

4. Explain the use of key words in Ruth.

The author of Ruth uses key words, like "lads" and "empty" to show how God restores Naomi's "lads" with a "lad" (1:5; 4:16) and fills her "empty" hands with grain (1:21; 3:17). Ruth places her trust in Yahweh and is protected by His "wings"

(2:12), and the Lord provides Boaz, who spreads his "wing" over Ruth (3:9).

5. What is *hesed?*

The Hebrew word *hesed* is translated "lovingkindness," "mercy," or "kindness," and it refers to covenant loyalty. Throughout the book of Ruth, the Lord demonstrates His covenant loyalty to Israel even in hopeless situations His kindness overflows.

6. What are the duties of a "near relative"? How does Boaz fulfill these? In what ways does he go beyond them?

The "near relative" or "kinsman-redeemer" is supposed to redeem land and slaves and take care of a brother's widow. Boaz does all of these things and more. Not only does he allow Ruth to glean in his fields, but he also gives special instructions to his men to leave extra grain behind for her to gather. He also invites her to share his meal (2:14–16). In all of this Boaz shows himself to be like the Lord, overflowing with kindness and mercy.

7. How does Ruth reflect the change from the time of judges to the time of kings?

Though Ruth begins in the time of the judges, it ends with a genealogy of King David and points the way to a new phase of Israel's history. Though Israel serves idols and stumbles again and again, Yahweh will not abandon her. The message of Ruth shows that He will raise up a King to be her Husband.

THOUGHT QUESTIONS

1. Many Jewish commentators believe that Elimelech sins when he leaves the land. Is this a good interpretation? Note what kind of place Bethlehem is during the period of the judges (Judg. 17:7, 9; 19:1).

According to Judges, Bethlehem is noted as a place of wickedness and idolatry. Elimelech's flight is away from the cities of Israel that have become worse than the surrounding nations (Judg. 19:10–30).

2. Boaz is a type of Christ, saving Ruth and Naomi. In light of this, why is it important that Ruth is a Moabitess?

It shows that the Greater Son of David will save the Jews and the Gentiles and "make the two into one new man, thus establishing peace, and might reconcile them both in one body to God" (Eph. 2:15–16).

3. Ruth meets with Boaz at night on the "threshing floor" (Ruth 3:6). What light does this shed on 2 Chronicles 3:1?

Second Chronicles 3:1 says that the temple is built on the "threshing floor" of Araunah. The threshing floor, the place where the wheat and the chaff are separated, is the foundation of the place where Israel worships. The connection with Ruth and Boaz means that the threshing floor is also a "trysting place" between Yahweh and His bride.

4. How many generations are there from Judah to David (Ruth 4:18–22)? Explain the significance of this, referring to Genesis 38 and Deuteronomy 23:2.

There are ten generations from Judah to David. According to Deuteronomy 23:2, ten generations are required for a bastard to be able to re-enter the assembly of Israel. Because of Judah's sin with Tamar (Gen. 38), the tribe of Judah is excluded from the leadership of Israel until David's generation.

"The Glory Departs": *1 Samuel 1–3*

REVIEW QUESTIONS [pages 122–126]

1. Who is being contrasted in 1 Samuel 2? How are they contrasted?

The contrast is between faithful Samuel and Eli's unfaithful sons, Hophni and Phinehas. Samuel is "adopted" into Eli's household and serves at the house of his Heavenly Father, while Eli's natural sons do not obey Yahweh or listen to the voice of their father (3:6, 16). Samuel ministers to the Lord (2:11b) while Eli's sons plunder the Lord's offerings (2:17). Samuel is "growing," which means "becoming great," while the sins of Eli's sons are growing "very great" (2:17).

2. What are the sins of Eli's sons?

Two main sins of Eli's sons are mentioned: First, they sin against the sacrifices. Instead of taking the portions of meat ascribed to them in the Law (Lev. 7:28–34; Deut. 18:1–5), they greedily take whatever they can get (1 Sam. 2:14). Also, they don't wait to burn the fat before grabbing their meal. Fat is the Lord's portion, the portion known as Yahweh's "bread." Eli's sons do not give the Lord His portion first; they serve the Lord only after serving themselves.

Second, they commit adultery with the women who serve the tabernacle (2:22). In Leviticus, adultery is connected with idolatry, and the fact that women are being violated in the tabernacle is a sign that the tabernacle itself is being violated.

3. What does the man of God say will happen to Eli's house? To the tabernacle at Shiloh?

The man of God says that Eli's house will be cut off from the altar so that they will no longer do altar service or share in the sacrifices. Also, the Lord promises that no one in Eli's family will see old age. On the other hand, the Lord promises to raise up a faithful priest who will lead an "enduring house." This priest is Zadok, who replaces Abiathar, the last priest in the line of Eli. Concerning the tabernacle, the man of God says that Eli will see the distress of Yahweh's dwelling. Shiloh is devastated by the Philistines and the ark is taken captive, never to return to the tabernacle of Moses.

4. Why does the man of God talk to Eli instead of Hophni and Phinehas?

The judgment of God falls on Eli because, even though he had not sinned like his sons, he honored his sons above God, and he has received benefits from his sons' wickedness.

5. Explain the play on the words "weight" and "honor" in 1 Samuel 3–4.

Eli had become "fat" because he benefited from his sons' abuse of the Lord's offerings and did not demand that the fat be given to the Lord. Ultimately, it is this "weight" that ends up killing Eli when he falls off his seat (4:18). In the Hebrew, there is a pun on the "honor" that Eli shows to his sons and his "heaviness." Both are based on the Hebrew word *kabad,* which often means "glorify." Eli treats God "lightly" and gives "weight" to his sons. By giving weight to his sons, he makes himself "weighty" with the fat of the Lord's offerings, but this very "weightiness" will mean his death.

THOUGHT QUESTIONS

1. What is Hannah promising in 1 Samuel 1:11? Compare Judges 13:1–7.

Hannah is promising to dedicate her son to Yahweh as a lifelong Nazarite just as Samson was. In Judges 13:1–7, the wife of Manoah is barren. The angel of the Lord comes and tells her she will give birth and the child will be a Nazarite to God from the womb until death. Hannah is not told to dedicate her son to Yahweh; nevertheless, she vows to offer him as a gift to the Lord if He would only remember her and give her a child.

2. Hannah is a barren woman who gives birth to a son. Yet, her song of celebration talks about the Lord overthrowing the rich and powerful and raising up the poor and weak. Why?

The barren woman giving birth is a picture of life coming from death. When Yahweh brings life from death the "world" is overturned. Hannah's song is about the social "resurrection" that is pictured in the birth of her son. When the barren gives birth, the poor and the oppressed will be delivered. Note how Hannah's song anticipates Mary's Magnificat (Lk. 1:47–55).

3. How is Hannah's song connected to the man of God's prophecy to Eli? Compare 2:5, 36.

Hannah not only sings that the barren woman becomes fruitful but also that the one who has children languishes. This alludes to the house of Eli, which languishes and is dying. The house of Eli, being "great" in wickedness, will be destroyed. Hannah wants the world to be turned upside down—the humble and poor exalted and the rich and proud brought down. The man of God announces to Eli that Yahweh is doing just that: the barren woman's son will stand in the place of the "fat" priest and his rebellious sons, who hire themselves out as priests in order to receive bread to eat.

THE HOUSE OF DAVID AND THE HOUSE OF YAHWEH

The Distress of My Dwelling: *1 Samuel 3–6*

REVIEW QUESTIONS [pages 129–135]

1. Explain how the books of Samuel follow the story of the Lord's house.

First and 2 Samuel tell the story of the end of one house of God and the beginning of a new house. In the first half, God judges Eli's house and brings distress to His own house. The Philistine captivity of the ark marks the end of the Mosaic tabernacle and the beginning of the end of Eli's house. Then 2 Samuel tells how the Lord begins to rebuild His house through His promise to build David's house.

2. How is the story of the capture of the ark like the Exodus from Egypt? How is it different?

The Philistines, who are descended from the Egyptians, discover that plagues come upon them when they bring the ark to Philistia. And as He did to the Egyptian gods during the Exodus, Yahweh overthrows the gods of the Philistines. When the Philistines put the ark in the temple of Dagon, assuming that Dagon has triumphed over Yahweh, they find the image of Dagon shattered in pieces before the ark the next day.

Even though Israel is guilty of idolatry and Moses had promised that Yahweh would spew Israel out of the land if they were unfaithful to the terms of the covenant, Israel remains in the land and Yahweh goes into exile. Yahweh is taking the curses of the covenant upon Himself and in so doing defeats Israel's enemies. This is a foreshadowing of the Gospel: as Yaweh's "defeat" by Dagon turns out to be Dagon's defeat, so Jesus defeats both Satan and sin by His humiliation.

3. In what ways is Samuel like Moses?

Like Moses, Samuel has many different tasks and serves during the transition to a new period in Israel's history. He is the mediator of a "new covenant." Samuel is from the clan of Kohath, who are tasked with carrying the ark and the furniture of the tabernacle. Even though he is not technically a priest, Samuel cares for the tabernacle and the ark while the real priests, Eli and his sons, neglect it.

Samuel is also a prophet. Samuel delivers the word of the Lord, especially the word of judgment, to Eli's house and to all Israel. As with Moses, the Lord reveals Himself to Samuel and does not let His words fall (1 Sam. 3:19). Even though Eli is going blind (3:2; 4:15), Samuel is called a "seer" (9:19). As prophet, Samuel's words begin to build a new world in Israel—a new form of government and a new order of worship.

Like Moses, Samuel is a military leader, leading Israel in repentance before the battle of Ebenezer (7:3–4). Finally, Samuel is a judge (7:15–17), the last and greatest of Israel's judges.

4. Explain the structure of 1 Samuel 4–7. What is important about it?

The structure of 1 Samuel 4–7 shows Samuel as a military leader:

A. Israel defeated by Philistines at Battle of Aphek (4:1–10)
   B. Ark taken and Eli's house destroyed (4:11–22)
      C. Yahweh fights Dagon in Philistia (5:1–12)
   B'. Ark returned (6:1–7:2)
A'. Israel victorious over the Philistines at Battle of Ebenezer (7:3–14)

In the first battle Israel uses the ark as a charm and, because of their idolatry, they are defeated and the ark is taken into captivity by the Philistines. Before the final battle of Ebenezer, Samuel leads Israel in repentance. The people confess their sins, put away their idols, and gather to renew the covenant at Mizpah. When Israel is led by a true "priest," Yahweh breaks out against Israel's enemies and gives them victory.

5. What are the rules for Israel's king in Deuteronomy?

In Deuteronomy 17:14–20, the rules for Israel's king are:

1. He must not multiply horses and chariots, which are used to conquer other nations. They may trade with other nations, but they are not to establish an empire beyond the land that the Lord had promised.
2. The king is not allowed to multiply wives because foreign wives will turn his heart away to follow other gods.
3. The king must not multiply gold and silver or live in luxury. Excessive wealth will tempt the king to think he is above his fellow countrymen and exempt himself from the requirements of the Law.

6. What is wrong with the elders' request for a king?

The elders' request reveals that their desire for a "king like the other nations" is a rejection of the Lord's rule over them. They want a new king who will "go out before us and fight our battles" (1 Sam. 8:9–20), even though the Lord has already promised to fight for Israel if they will only obey Him.

7. Explain the changing meaning of "judgment" in Samuel's speech.

The Hebrew word *mishpat* usually means "judgment." When Samuel tells Israel that he is going to discuss the "judgment" of the king, they expect him to talk about the king's justice. Instead, Samuel talks about the "habits" of the king that are anything but just. As Samuel's speech continues, it becomes clear that the king *is* a judgment upon Israel for rejecting their rightful King. The elders ask for a king "who may judge us," and that is exactly what Yahweh gives them: a king who brings "judgment."

8. According to Samuel, what is Israel's king going to do?

Samuel emphasizes that the king is going to "take" (used six times: 1 Sam. 8:11, 13, 14, 15, 16, 17) from the people. He will take sons for the army, daughters to serve in his household, fields to give to his friends, as well as servants and work animals. The king will also make himself like God and demand a tenth of Israel's increase. Throughout the message is clear: rejecting Yahweh is like going back to Egypt. Only now when Israel cries out for deliverance, Yahweh will not raise up deliverers as He did before (8:18). Now Israel must live with her kings.

THOUGHT QUESTIONS

1. When the Israelites bring the ark into the camp at the battle of Aphek, it is called the "ark of the covenant of Yahweh of hosts who sits above the cherubim" (4:4). Why is this elaborate description used here?

There is irony in this description. "Hosts" means "armies," and Israel brings the ark into battle thinking that the armies of the Lord accompany it. No doubt they expected to see the glory cloud appear between the cherubim. However, because of Eli and his sons' disobedience, the armies of heaven fight *against* Israel instead of *for* her.

2. Why is it significant that Eli dies by falling from his seat (4:13–18)?

Eli is sitting at the gates of the city (v. 18), an act which symbolizes his authority and rule in Israel. When he falls from his seat, it is a picture of the "unseating" of his family from leadership in Israel just as the Lord had promised (2:27–36).

3. The ark of God goes into "exile" in Philistia, and when it returns it is filled with gold (6:4). How does this fit with other "exile" or "exodus" stories?

> Whenever God's people go into "exile" in a foreign country, they always leave richer than when they entered. Think of Abraham in Egypt (Gen. 12:10–20), Moses in Egypt (Exod. 11:2; 12:35–36), Jacob serving Laban (Gen. 31:1–13), and David among the Philistines (1 Sam. 27–30).

4. What happens to the men of Beth-shemesh when the ark returns there (6:19–21)? What does this tell us about the righteousness of Israel at the time? Are they any better than the Philistines?

> When the ark returns to Israel from the Philistines, the men of Beth-shemesh initially offer sacrifices but some desecrate the ark by looking into it. Because of this Yahweh sends a plague and 50,070 men are struck down. This proves that Israel is no different than the Philistines, who were judged with a plague of mice, tumors, and death (5:6–12).

5. When the elders of Israel ask for a king, the Lord says that this is "like all the deeds which they have done since the day that I brought them up from Egypt to this day—in that they have forsaken Me and served other gods" (8:8). How is the request for a king an act of idolatry?

> Israel's request for a king is first and foremost a *rejection* of the Lord's rule over them. It is an act of idolatry because the king stands in Yahweh's place and represents Israel's desire to be free of His lordship.

'Tis Like Another Fall of Man: *1 Samuel 9–15*

REVIEW QUESTIONS [pages 136–140]

1. What is Saul doing when he first appears in 1 Samuel? What does that tell us about Saul?

When we first meet Saul (1 Sam. 9:3ff), he is looking for his father's donkeys. Saul is a faithful son who cares about his father's animals. This is a good sign because Hophni and Phinehas had both been rebellious sons. Initially Saul is more like Samuel, and this is a hopeful sign for Israel.

2. What does Saul look like? What does that tell us about him?

Saul is a handsome man and a head taller than any other Israelite (9:2). Since the Bible often uses physical descriptions to indicate inner qualities (i.e., Esau is "hairy," which is his outward glory but is also beastlike; Absalom is "handsome," which occasions his pride and vanity), Saul's size and good looks indicate that he has the appearance of a king. Note the similar descriptions of Joseph (Gen. 39:6) and David (1 Sam. 16:12).

3. In what ways is Saul like Gideon?

Like Gideon, Saul is initially a humble man. He does not seek to be king. Saul also wonders why he has been chosen since he comes from the smallest tribe of Israel, Benjamin (1 Sam. 9:21). When Israel gathers to anoint him king, Saul hides in the baggage (10:22). He also is humble after his first victory and refuses to harm those who formerly opposed his kingship (11:12–13). In so doing, he follows the example of Moses (Num. 12:3) and does not return evil for evil.

4. What is Saul's first sin? How does this sin make Saul like a king of the nations?

Saul sins by not waiting for Samuel to offer sacrifice. Samuel told Saul to wait seven days, but Saul, fearing the army will scatter, goes ahead and offers an ascension offering by himself. When Samuel confronts him, Saul blames the people (1 Sam. 13:11–12), as Aaron blamed the people for the golden calf. Saul's sin strikes at the heart of what it means to be a king: the king of Israel is to be directed by the word of the Lord, which comes through the prophet and the priest.

5. What is Saul's second sin?

Saul's second sin is against his army and his son Jonathan (1 Sam. 14). Saul rashly forbids his army to eat during battle and prevents Israel from slaughtering the Philistines. When Jonathan eats some honey at the end of the battle, Saul wants to kill his son for violating his command. Saul has clearly changed: he is ready to kill his heroic son because he ignored a foolish command. His mistreatment of his army makes Saul more like a king of the Gentile nations.

6. Explain the connections between Gideon's battle with the Midianites and Saul's battle at Michmash.

There are a number of important similarities between Gideon's battle with the Midianites and Saul's battle at Michmash. In both, the Israelites fearfully hide in caves (Judg. 6:2; 1 Sam. 13:6). In both battles, the Lord sets Israel's enemies against each other (Judg. 7:22; 1 Sam. 14:20). Both enemies are as numerous as the sand on the seashore (Judg. 7:12; 1 Sam. 13:5). However, Saul doesn't remember the example of Gideon, who won with only three hundred men, and is afraid with his six hundred men (1 Sam. 13:15). Instead Saul wants to kill his valiant son Jonathan, who thinks that they don't need great numbers to be victorious. Saul is acting more like Abimelech, the "bramble king" who was the son of Gideon.

7. What is Saul's third sin?

Saul's final fall occurs when he doesn't carry out the ban of holy war God decreed against the Amalekites (see Exod. 17:8–16; Deut. 25:17–19). Instead of destroying everything,

Saul spares the best of the flocks and herds as well as the Amalekite king, Agag.

8. How are Saul's sins like the sins of Genesis 3–6?

Saul commits sin in each of the areas of the earth described in Genesis: garden, land, and world. In the "garden," Saul sins by sacrificing without waiting for Samuel. He sins in the "land" when he makes his soldiers fast during battle and then seeks to kill Jonathan. Finally, he sins in the "world" when he spares Agag and the plunder of the Amalekites. After his sin, Saul is like Adam and blames the "bride," Israel, rather than taking responsibility for his sin. In these sins, Saul is another Adam and Cain and is also like the sons of God (Gen. 6).

9. Explain how Saul becomes like Abimelech.

Saul is like Abimelech in a couple of ways. Saul slaughters the priests of Nob who had helped David (1 Sam. 22). Only one escapes, just as only one of Abimelech's brothers escapes from a similar slaughter (Judg. 9). Saul asks one of his soldiers to put an end to his life after he is wounded in battle so that it will not be said that the "uncircumcised" had killed him. Abimelech likewise asks his armor-bearer to run him through so that it would not be said that he had been killed by a woman (Judg. 9:45).

THOUGHT QUESTIONS

1. As Saul goes to meet Samuel, he comes across some young women at a well (1 Sam. 9:11–13). How is this similar to scenes in Genesis 24 and 29? How is it different? Why is it different?

In Genesis 24 and 29, "well scenes" lead to marriages, so when Saul meets a woman at a well, we are led to expect a marriage. What follows is Saul's anointing as king. Saul is being "betrothed" to Israel and the well scene lends a marital context to Saul's anointing.

CHAPTER 4: THE HOUSE OF DAVID AND THE HOUSE OF YAHWEH** 61

2. What is Samuel going to do when Saul first meets him (1 Sam. 9:11–14)? In the light of Deuteronomy 12, is this a lawful thing for Samuel to do?

According to 1 Samuel 9:11–14, Samuel is going to offer a sacrifice on the local high place. Deuteronomy 12 says that sacrifices should only be offered "in the place which the Lord your God shall choose for His name to dwell." The key is to realize that the terms of Deuteronomy 12 are only in force when there is a sanctuary of the Lord that is operative. However, in Samuel's day the sanctuary of the Lord had been destroyed by the Philistines. Israel is in a kind of exile, even though they are in their own land.

3. What is Saul's hometown (1 Sam. 10:26)? What happened in this town before Saul's time (Judg. 19–20)? Why does the Lord choose a man from this town as the first king?

Saul is from Gibeah. In Judges, Gibeah is one of the locations of that manifests extraordinary corruption, like that of Sodom and Gomorrah. Just as Yahweh chose people who were "least of all" (Deut. 7:7), so He also chooses a king from one of the most despised cities in Israel. This also reminds us of Jesus who comes from Nazareth (Jn. 1:46)

4. Saul receives the Spirit and becomes a new man (1 Sam. 10:6–13). Was he saved? See 1 Samuel 16:14.

This is a difficult reality: In 1 Samuel 10 the Spirit makes Saul a "new man," but later when Saul hardens himself in disobedience, the Spirit leaves him. This same thing is in view in John 15 when Jesus says that branches that have been attached to the vine are cut off and cast into the fire. Saul is a member of God's covenant people in a real way, but he also does not persevere and it is ultimately "cut out."

5. How does Samuel's statement in 1 Samuel 15:23 foreshadow Saul's future (see 1 Sam. 28)? How is rebellion like "divination"?

According to Samuel, rebellion and "divination" stem from a common source—rejecting the word of the Lord. In 1 Samuel 15, Saul is guilty of rebellion, but Samuel is showing that rebellion is like idolatry because it involves serving a "different" god. Saul's later visit to the witch at Endor (1 Sam. 28) confirms Samuel's words.

Humility Before Honor:
1 Samuel 25, 2 Samuel 6, 11–12

REVIEW QUESTIONS [pages 141–152]

1. How is David like Saul? How does David's battle with Goliath show that he is superior to Saul?

Like Saul, David has the "looks" of a king, which picture his character (1 Sam. 16:12–13). David also receives Spirit of God at his anointing (16:13). However, David's battle with Goliath shows that David is a better man than Saul. Though he is a youth, David is unafraid of the giant's taunts while Saul is filled with fear (though he too is a "giant"). Saul gives David his armor, but David refuses to wear it (17:38–39), putting his confidence instead in the strength of the Lord.

2. How does David treat Saul when Saul is persecuting him?

Even while he is crown prince, David does not rebel in order to take the throne. Though he is given two separate opportunities to kill Saul, David will not "take" the kingdom by disobediently harming the "Lord's anointed."

3. What is the significance of the incident with Nabal and Abigail?

The incident shows that David's patience with Saul will be rewarded. Rather than taking vengeance into his own hands, David waits for the Lord to deal with Nabal. When Nabal dies, David inherits Nabal's land and wife, Abigail. The same will happen with Saul.

4. What does David do after he conquers Jerusalem?

After David conquers Jerusalem, he decides to set up the throne of Yahweh there. This is an important moment in restoring the house of God that was ruined by the sins of Eli's sons. A new stage of Israel's history begins here with the building of a new house for Yahweh, the "tabernacle of David."

5. What is the difference between the worship of the Mosaic tabernacle and the worship of the Davidic tabernacle?

The clearest difference between Mosaic and Davidic worship is the role of music and song. In Leviticus, almost nothing is said during worship at the Mosaic tabernacle. While burnt animal offerings are still presented by the descendants of Zadok, Davidic worship is crowned by the Levitical orchestra and psalm-singing.

6. How is the covenant with David like the covenant with Abraham? In what ways is it different?

God's covenant with David is an extension of the covenant He made with Abraham. Like Abraham, David's son will have a great name, for he will build a temple that connects heaven and earth. David, like Abraham, is given a land for Israel to rest in (2 Sam. 7:11). Just as Abraham is promised that Yahweh will defend him, blessing those who bless him and cursing those who curse him, so David is promised victory over his enemies. And finally, Abraham is told that his seed would bless all nations, and David learns that this seed will come from him.

But the covenant with David also goes beyond God's covenant with Abraham. Now the Lord promises that Israel will be stable and secure in the land (7:10), that God will give them a permanent dynasty—a Davidic dynasty ruled by a king of peace (Shlomo/Solomon).

7. Explain the structure of the story of David and Bathsheba. How does this show that David's sin threatens the kingdom?

The story of David's sin with Bathsheba centers on Nathan's confrontation with David (2 Sam. 12:1–15a). Up to that point David had covered up his sin, but at Nathan's confrontation we are faced with the question of David's response: will he respond like Adam and Saul? David does not respond by blaming Bathsheba or the people of God. He confesses his sin, and as a result David keeps the kingdom. The narrative begins and ends with the siege of the city of Rabbah.

8. What is odd about David's mourning for his son? Why does he mourn this way?

David fasts and mourns while his son is sick, but when his son dies he cleans himself up and feasts! When we understand that the death of David's son is punishment for David's sin of murder, David's actions begins to make sense. If the Lord were just with David, David would have died for his crime. But David's son dies in David's place. When the child dies, David rises up to new life. This points to another "Son of David" who gave His life so that we could be raised up from the dust to feast at the Father's table.

THOUGHT QUESTIONS

1. When David is going out with the Philistines to fight Saul, they suspect he will turn and fight against them (1 Sam. 29:1–5). Are they right?

The Philistines are right to be suspicious of David. He has never raised his hand against Saul, why would he start now? Since David is on good terms with Achish, he is really stuck between two betrayals. However, the Philistines' suspicion of David, which results in his departure for Ziklag, is the means by which the Lord saves David from having to choose between loyalties.

2. What kind of men are the "sons of Zeruiah" (2 Sam. 3:39)? Who are they? Why doesn't David just get rid of them? Look at 1 Chronicles 2:16.

The "sons of Zeruiah"—Abshai, Joab, and Asahel—give David continual grief because of their rash, impulsive actions. But they were David's nephews, the sons of his sister, Zeruiah (1 Chr. 2:16), and therefore David does not get rid of them.

3. Second Samuel 10 records David's victory over the Ammonites. Why is this story placed here? Compare 1 Samuel 11 in context.

In 2 Samuel 10, a parallel is drawn between David and Saul. Saul was victorious over the Ammonites early in his career and then fell into sin. When David similarly defeats the Ammonites, the text invites the question, "Will David fall into sin like Saul?" The answer is chapter 11.

4. During the rebellion of Absalom, David leaves the land and returns when Absalom is defeated. How is this "exodus" similar to and different from other exodus stories?

As in other "exodus" stories (Gen. 12:10–20; Exod. 12:33–40), David leaves the land under threat and eventually returns to establish a "new" kingdom. However, David doesn't return to the land enriched, which is the normal pattern in exodus stories.

5. Second Samuel 20:23–26 lists the officials of David's court, but they have already been listed in 2 Samuel 8:15–18. Why are they listed again?

The officials of David's court are listed again in 2 Samuel 20 because David's kingdom had to be reestablished after Absalom's rebellion.

Son of David: *1 Kings 1–11*

REVIEW QUESTIONS

1. Why does Solomon ask for wisdom?

Solomon asks the Lord for wisdom so that he will be able to rule well as a king and judge the people rightly.

2. How is Solomon's wisdom connected to Adam?

Solomon requests "to know good and evil," which reminds us of Adam and the tree in the garden of Eden. Adam did not know good and evil, and he was not allowed to eat from the tree of "judgment." However, God grants Solomon's request, showing that he has moved beyond Adam.

3. In what ways is Solomon's reign a fulfillment of promises to Abraham?

God promised Abraham that his seed would be a blessing to the Gentiles. All the nations of the earth seek and are blessed by Solomon's wisdom (1 Kgs. 10:23–25). God promised Abraham and his seed a land where they would live in peace and safety. During Solomon's rule this comes to pass (4:20, 25). The borders of the land during Solomon's reign are the borders promised to Abraham (Gen. 15:18; 1 Kgs. 4:21). Also the promise that Abraham's descendants would be like the sand on the seashore and like the stars in heaven happens under Solomon (1 Kgs. 3:8; 4:20). God promised Abraham that He would be God to him and his descendants and live among them. Solomon builds a permanent house for God's name in the land of Israel.

4. How is the temple different from the tabernacle?

The tabernacle's furnishings, glorious as they were, were mainly visible only from the inside. From the outside, all that was visible was the goat-hair covering. The temple's beauty was much more outward. The greatness of Solomon's temple was plain to everyone who saw it. One of the other major differences is the inclusion of the king's house into the temple area. Before this the Lord never shared His house, but now Solomon lives "in" the Lord's house, as a prince over Israel.

5. What three sins does Solomon commit?

Solomon violates all three of the Lord's commands to kings in Deuteronomy 17. Solomon gathers a large number of horses and chariots (1 Kgs. 10:26), and brings even more from Egypt (10:28). He collects a staggering number of gold talents (666!) each year (10:14). And finally Solomon, like the sons of God in Genesis 6, marries foreign women who turn his heart to foreign gods (11:1–8).

6. What happens to Israel because of Solomon's sins?

Because of Solomon's sins, Israel is ultimately torn in two (1 Kgs. 11:9–13; 26–40).

THOUGHT QUESTIONS

1. Explain the location of the story about the two harlots and the child (1 Kgs. 3:16–28). Why is it here?

This story immediately follows Solomon's request for wisdom that he might rule Yahweh's people well. It shows that Solomon's request has been granted him. The gift of divine wisdom, which the people saw in Solomon, enables him to "divide" the righteous from the unrighteous, for God had inspired him for the government of His people.

2. How does Solomon reorganize Israel (1 Kgs. 4:7–19)?

Rather than following the tribal boundaries set up at the time of Joshua, Solomon organizes Israel into twelve districts.

3. Compare the two dreams of Solomon (1 Kgs. 3:1–15 and 9:1–9). Compare the two encounters with Hiram of Tyre (5:1–15 and 9:10–14). How

are these similar scenes different? What does this say about Solomon's reign?

Solomon's first dream contains promises from the Lord while the second is more threatening. Likewise, Solomon's dealings with Hiram of Tyre begin well but turn bad later on. Both of these point to the fact that Solomon's reign has begun to decline.

4. The account of the building of the temple is at the center of 1–2 Chronicles. This differs in a marked way from 1–2 Kings. What does this suggest about the purpose of those books? Note especially 2 Chronicles 36:22–23.

The purpose of 1 and 2 Kings is to remind Israel why they entered captivity and therefore, the prophets are central to book's message. On the other hand, 1 and 2 Chronicles is meant to encourage the people to rebuild the temple after the exile, which is why the temple is central.

5. The center of Solomon's prayer in 1 Kings 8 is about plagues in the land (vv. 37–40). Why is this central? As a clue, notice how 6:1 dates the construction of the temple.

Solomon began to build the temple in the 480th year after the exodus. The reference to plagues reminds us of Egypt. Solomon is reminding Israel that if they return to "Egyptian" practices and fail to keep covenant with Yahweh, the plagues of Egypt will overtake them.

CHAPTER 5

WALKING IN THE CUSTOMS OF THE NATIONS

The Garment Torn: *1 Kings 11–12*

REVIEW QUESTIONS [pages 161–166]

1. How are the books of Kings a "reverse" of the books of Samuel?

First and 2 Samuel move from a distressed tabernacle to a new temple, while 1–2 Kings moves from the newly constructed temple to its destruction.

2. Explain the order of the story of the Northern Kingdom in 1–2 Kings.

The story of the Northern Kingdom is divided into two halves. Both halves tell the story of seven kings, a story that begins with a king named Jeroboam and ends with a king whose reign is a terrible disaster. In between these two narratives is sandwiched the stories of Elijah and Elisha (1 Kgs. 17:1–2 Kgs. 13:21).

3. Why is the kingdom of Solomon divided?

The kingdom was divided because Solomon's son, Rehoboam, foolishly makes the yoke his father has placed on the people even heavier despite their request for relief (1 Kgs. 12:12–15).

4. Give some examples of the power of a prophet's word in 1–2 Kings.

Ahijah prophesies that the kingdom of Israel will be torn in two (1 Kgs. 11:26–40), and it happens. When Solomon dismisses Abiathar from serving as priest, the word of the Lord is fulfilled against Eli (1 Kgs. 2:27). The Lord hardens the heart of Rehoboam, fulfilling the words of Ahijah (12:15). During the reign of Ahab, "Hiel the Bethelite built Jericho," and his firstborn and youngest sons both die, just as Joshua promised would happen to anyone who tried to rebuild Jericho (1 Kgs. 16:34; Josh. 6:26). Many prophets also warn that Israel and Judah will be driven from the land unless they repent, and this comes true (2 Kgs. 24:2).

5. Why does Jeroboam set up golden calves?

Jeroboam sets up two golden calves in Bethel to protect his power by keeping the Northern tribes from traveling to Judah to worship in Jerusalem.

6. What commandment does Jeroboam break?

Jeroboam breaks the second commandment by using images to worship Yahweh. The sin of worshiping Yahweh through golden calves becomes the archetypal sin that the Northern Kingdom repeats for its whole history (cf. 1 Kgs. 15:29–30, 34; 16:18–19, 26).

7. Why does Jeroboam choose Bethel for one of his shrines?

Bethel was the place where Jacob set up an altar to worship Yahweh. Jeroboam is making the case that the Northern tribes are the true sons of Jacob and that his institution of worship in Bethel is "nothing new."

8. How is the punishment for breaking the second commandment seen in the books of Kings?

The judgment promised to those who violate the second commandment is that they will be punished to the third or fourth generations. This is exactly what happens to the kings of the Northern Kingdom. Nearly all of them last only a couple of generations. Eventually the Northern Kingdom's series of houses are "swept clean" (1 Kgs. 14:10; 21:21).

THOUGHT QUESTIONS

1. The prophet Ahijah is called a "Shilonite" (1 Kgs. 11:29; 14:2). Why is this significant?

Shiloh is the place where the tabernacle was destroyed and where the priestly line of Eli came to an end. Ahijah is going to announce the end of a royal dynasty (Jeroboam's house).

2. A "man of God from Judah" prophesies that Jeroboam's altar in Bethel will be defiled by Josiah (1 Kgs. 13:1–2). This is fulfilled in 2 Kings 23:15–16. How does this fit with the larger themes of the books of Kings?

There are many years between the man of God's prophecy and its fulfillment. This emphasizes the power of the Lord's prophets; not one of their words will fall to the ground.

3. Why is the man of God from Judah eaten by a lion (1 Kgs. 13:20–25)?

The man of God from Judah is eaten by a lion when he disobeys the word of the Lord not to eat or drink anything on his way home. This foreshadows what the "lion" from the tribe of Judah, Josiah, will do to those who worship other gods (2 Kgs. 22:16–20; 23:1–27).

4. Jeroboam's son Abijah gets sick in 1 Kings 14:1. What does the sickness of the king's son represent? What does the boy's death represent (14:6–16)?

The sickness of the king's son represents the sickness of Jeroboam's dynasty and kingdom. His son's death represents the "clean sweep" Yahweh is going to perform on Jeroboam's house (14:10).

5. Yahweh tells Baasha that He raised him from the "dust" to be king (1 Kgs. 16:2). Discuss this in light of Genesis 2:7.

The reference to Genesis 2:7 points out that Baasha was given an opportunity to be a "New Adam." But, like the old Adam, Baasha disobeyed the word of the Lord.

Return to Canaan: *1 Kings 17–2 Kings 4*
Aftershocks in Judah: *2 Kings 9–12*

REVIEW QUESTIONS [pages 167–178]

1. What does the Bible tell us about the reign of Omri?

First Kings mentions that Omri builds up Samaria and makes it the capital of the Northern Kingdom. But mainly Omri is noted as the king who "did evil in the sight of Yahweh, and acted more wickedly than all who were before him" (1 Kgs. 16:25).

2. What made Ahab's reign worse than any other?

All of Ahab's actions—rebuilding the altars and shrines of the Canaanites, marrying Jezebel, a Sidonian princess (Sidon was the first born son of Canaan; Gen. 10:15), and rebuilding the city of Jericho—are all attempts to undo the conquest of Joshua.

3. What was Ahab trying to do? How can you tell?

Ahab is trying to reunite the Northern and Southern kingdoms under the house of Omri with a temple of Baal at the center. To this end he makes an alliance with Jehoshaphat, king of Judah. Jehoshaphat's son, Jehoram, marries Ahab and Jezebel's daughter, Athaliah, and in the events that follow, North and South get all mixed up, making this section of Kings difficult to sort out.

4. Explain how Elijah and Elisha are like Moses and Joshua.

Like Moses and Joshua, they lead the people out of "Egypt," renew the covenant, and conquer the land, driving out Ahab's "Canaanites." Like Moses, Elijah goes into exile where he meets a woman and "gives" her a son (Exod. 2:23; 1 Kgs. 17:17–24). Elijah's actions on Mount Carmel remind us of the plagues of Egypt and the Passover, as well as the covenant on Sinai (Exod. 12:12; 32:27; 1 Kgs. 18:27, 40). Both Moses and Elijah ask the Lord to take their lives after Israel's idolatry (Exod. 32:31–32; 1 Kgs. 19:4). After Elijah is refreshed, he travels forty days and nights to Horeb, where the Lord appears to him and the same place where the glory of the Lord passed by Moses (Exod. 33:17–34:9, 28; 1 Kgs. 19:8–14).

Elijah also departs in a way that resembles Moses' death. No one knows where Moses is buried, and a party searches for Elijah but can't find him (Deut. 34:6; 2 Kgs. 2:15–18). Both Moses and Elijah name their successors by transferring their "spirit" to them (Num. 27:15–23; 2 Kgs. 2:9–14, 23–25; cf. vv. 1–6). Finally, if Elijah is a new Moses, Elisha is a new Joshua. He is a servant to Elijah, as Joshua was to Moses. When Elijah leaves in 2 Kings 2, Elisha receives a double portion of his spirit, the portion of the firstborn, and continues Elijah's ministry. Like Joshua, Elisha enacts a "reconquest" of the land, and though he calls down judgment (2 Kgs. 2:23–25), his ministry, unlike Joshua's, is mainly a ministry of mercy, not destruction.

5. Who is Jehu? What did he do?

Jehu is anointed by Elisha as the avenger against the house of Ahab. His job is to "cut off from Ahab every male person both bond and free in Israel," and to kill Jezebel as well (2 Kgs. 9:1–13). Jehu gets around: he kills Joram of Israel, kills Jezebel in Samaria, kills the seventy sons of Ahab, and gathers the worshipers of Baal into the temple in Samaria and slaughters them all.

6. What effect does Jehu's attack on Ahab's house have on Judah?

Since the Northern and Southern kingdoms are so entwined at this time, Jehu also creates problems for the Southern kingdom. He kills Ahaziah, the king of Judah (2 Kgs. 9:27), and forty-two members of Ahaziah's household (10:12–14). He provides a painful lesson to Judah: if you get too close to the Northern Kingdom, you'll be punished in the same way.

7. Who is Athaliah? What makes her reign different?

Athaliah is the daughter of Ahab and Jezebel. In 2 Kings 11, she takes over Jerusalem when she discovers that her son, Ahaziah, is dead. She then tries to destroy all the royal offspring (only Joash survives) and sets herself up as queen. However, 2 Kings does recognize her rule with the normal royal formula (2 Kgs. 11:1–3). She bursts in as a surprise and interrupts the story of David's kingdom and nearly brings it to an end.

8. How is the family of David restored to the throne of Judah?

Joash, the last son of Ahaziah, is saved from Athaliah's destruction. He is raised up as a new Moses, and his coronation is also a covenant-ceremony. Joash is given a copy of the testimony and begins his reign by purging Judah of Baal worship.

9. How is Joash like Solomon?

Both are made kings after overcoming an opponent (1 Kgs. 1; 2 Kgs. 11). Both Joash and Solomon reign for forty years. The descriptions of their coronation ceremonies are both very similar (1 Kgs. 1:38–40; 2 Kgs. 11:9–12). Joash is also called "the king's son," which refers to the fact that he was brought up in the temple. Though he is an orphan, God is his true Father. The "king's son" means that Joash is both David's son and the "son of God," a title God promised to give Solomon (2 Sam. 7:14).

10. What does Joash do after Jehoiada's death?

According to Chronicles, when Jehoiada dies, Joash goes back to worshiping the gods of his mother (2 Chr. 24:18). When he is confronted about it, he puts Zechariah, the son of Jehoiada, to death.

THOUGHT QUESTIONS

1. At Carmel, Elijah sets up an altar of twelve stones, which is consumed by fire from heaven (1 Kgs. 18:30–40). What does this signify?

The altar represents the twelve tribes of Israel, the northern kingdom of ten tribes, and the two tribes of the southern kingdom. There was no fire under the sacrifice and it was drenched with water. The sacrifice is consumed by the fire of the living God in the place of Israel. It acts as a substitution.

2. Ahab fights a battle against the Arameans, but he spares the Aramean king, Ben-hadad (1 Kgs. 20:26–34). Compare to 1 Samuel 15. What does this suggest about Ahab? See also 1 Kings 22:34 and 1 Samuel 31:3.

It suggests that Ahab is following the example of Saul and will have a similar end. In 1 Kings 20:26–34, Ahab spares the Aramean king, Ben-hadad, just as Saul spared the Amalekite king, Agag, in 1 Samuel 15. Finally, both kings are wounded by arrows, wounds which ultimately end in their deaths.

3. How does the Lord entice Ahab to his death (1 Kgs. 22:13–23)? Is this fair?

Since Ahab will not listen to the Word of the Lord, Micaiah the prophet tells Ahab what he wants to hear. God is dealing crookedly with the crooked, just as He promised (Ps. 18:26).

4. Remember Elijah's exile among the Gentiles. How does Elisha's aid to Naaman fit with this (2 Kgs. 5)? Who is Naaman? What effect will his recovery have on Israel?

Naaman is a powerful Syrian general who has defeated Israel a number of times before. It would be better for Israel if Naaman died, but Elisha heals him. As Daniel would do later, Elisha helps Israel's enemies. It also foreshadows the New Testament. Israel's judgment becomes a blessing to the Gentiles.

5. Second Kings 8:1–6 is a story about the woman whose son Elisha has raised from the dead. How does this story fit with the rest of the story about this woman?

The widow is a picture of faithful Israel. Earlier, she received Elisha and her son was raised from the dead. Second Kings 8:1–6 is an exile and return (exodus) story. Again the widow represents Israel, who will go into exile and return to have her land restored.

Assyrian Threat: *2 Kings 17; Jonah 1–2*

REVIEW QUESTIONS [pages 179–186]

1. What nation is the great power during the final days of the Northern Kingdom?

Assyria.

2. When did Jonah live?

Jonah lived during the reign of Jeroboam II (2 Kgs. 14:25).

3. What was the condition of Israel during Jonah's life? How does this help us understand Jonah's flight?

Even though Jeroboam II is an evil king who leads Israel in the sins of the first Jeroboam, the Lord has mercy on Israel and restores some of the land other kings have lost. This is a fulfillment of the words of Jonah (2 Kgs. 14:24, 26). Assyria, during this period, is growing strong and becoming a real threat to Israel. When the Lord commands Jonah to go preach to the Assyrians in Nineveh, Jonah suspects that the only reason for this is ultimately because Yahweh wants to show mercy to the Assyrians (why else would He send a prophet?). This is hard pill for Jonah to swallow, because if the Lord has compassion on Assyria, Israel is in bigger trouble than ever.

4. What does the Lord threaten to do in Deuteronomy 32? How does this help us understand Jonah?

In Deuteronomy 32, the Lord promises that if Israel provokes Him to jealousy by serving other gods, He will turn His attention to other nations and provoke Israel to jealousy in return. Jonah knows this and is "provoked" by Yahweh's desire to show mercy on Israel's enemies.

5. What is Jonah fleeing from? How does the Lord turn this around?

Jonah is fleeing from the Lord's "presence" (1:3, 10) and thus from his calling to be a prophet. Prophets are supposed to "stand before the Lord" (1 Kgs. 17:1). However, even when Jonah flees, he ends up doing what the Lord calls him to do. When the ship Jonah is fleeing on encounters a storm, the crew begins crying out to their gods in fear. By the end of the storm, and because of Jonah's words, the men have turned from their gods and have begun to serve Yahweh. Even when Jonah is trying to avoid evangelizing Assyrians, the first thing he does is convert a boatload of pagan sailors.

6. How does Jonah's life picture the threat of exile?

When Jonah rebels against the word of the Lord, he ends up being cast into the sea, a kind of exile. So too will Israel be cast into the roaring "sea" of the Gentiles (Is. 5:30; 17:12–13, Ps. 65:7–8).

7. How does Jonah's life picture the promise of return from exile?

Yahweh doesn't let His prophet die in exile: He sends a great fish to save Jonah and spit him back out on dry land. Likewise Jeremiah describes Nebuchadnezzar and Babylon as a monster who swallows Israel (Jer. 51:34). But the Lord also promises to judge Bel, the god of Babylon, and make him vomit what he had swallowed. Like Jonah, once Israel has offered sacrifices of thanksgiving and pays her vows in the place of exile, the Lord will return them to the "dry" land. And as Jonah's exile gave life to a bunch of pagan sailors, so Israel's return will be life to the nations.

THOUGHT QUESTIONS

1. Why does Shalmanezer of Assyria take Hoshea away to prison (2 Kgs. 17:1–3)? What message should this send to the Southern Kingdom?

Shalmanezer carts Hoshea off to prison because he had been secretly seeking an alliance with So, king of Egypt. The Southern Kingdom should realize that seeking alliances (especially with Egypt) will not deliver them from judgment.

2. Who is brought into the Northern Kingdom after Israel has been removed (2 Kgs. 17:24)? What effect does this have on the spiritual climate in the North (2 Kgs. 17:34–41)?

The Assyrians bring in people from Babylon, Cuthah, Avva, Hamath, and Sepharvaim and settle them in Samaria. Every nation persisted in their former practices and made gods of their own and served them, while they claimed to be worshipping the Lord. The result is that their idolatrous practices (serving idols and worshipping the Lord) become customary to their grandchildren.

3. Amos the prophet is prophesying in the days of Jeroboam, the son of Joash, king of Israel (Amos 1:1). According to Amos, what sins characterize the Northern Kingdom (see 4:1–4)?

According to Amos, the idolatry of Israel is characterized by oppression of the poor and needy.

4. The book of Jonah is ordered as a "two-panel" story. Chapter three begins again where chapter one began. This suggests that there is a connection between the great fish of chapters one and two and the gourd in chapter four. What does the gourd represent?

The gourd and the fish are parallel with one another; both point to the Assyrian empire. The fish protected Jonah from drowning and death, like the ark. The gourd protects Jonah from the sun for a time, and then it withers. Just so, Assyria will be an umbrella over Israel (a kind of "ark") for a time, but then will rebel against Yahweh and leave Israel exposed to the heat of the "sun."

5. Whom does Nahum prophesy against (1:1)? Why? What has happened between the time of Jonah and the time of Nahum?

Nahum prophesies against Nineveh. Since Nineveh repented and turned to Yahweh during Jonah's ministry, the book of Nahum means that somewhere between Jonah and Nahum, the Assyrians apostatized.

CHAPTER 6

THE LAST DAYS OF JUDAH

A New David: *2 Kings 18–20; Isaiah 36–39*
The Book of the Law: *2 Kings 22–23*

REVIEW QUESTIONS [pages 189–195]

1. What was Judah supposed to learn from the fall of Israel?

The fall of Israel is a clear message to Judah: If you turn from the Lord, the Lord will remove you; instead of subduing your enemies, your enemies will subdue you; instead of receiving tribute, you will be forced to give tribute.

2. What does Hezekiah do during his reign?

He fights against the Philistines and he expands the lands of Judah. Additionally, Hezekiah restores true worship to the Southern Kingdom and is the first king to get rid of the places of worship on the "high places." He also destroys the Asherah pillars throughout the land and crushes the bronze serpent of Moses that Judah has been worshiping. Because of this the Lord protects Judah from the Assyrians (2 Kgs. 18–19; Is. 36–37).

3. How is Judah's deliverance from Assyria like the Passover?

Sennacherib's siege of Jerusalem reminds us of Pharaoh's oppression of Israel. The conflict is also clearly a contest between the gods of the Assyrians and Yahweh, just as when Pharaoh enslaves the seed in Egypt. In the end Yahweh humbles the gods of the Assyrians just as He did the gods of Egypt (Is. 37:21–29; Exod. 12:12). As at the Passover, the angel of the Lord goes through the Assyrian camp and kills 185,000 (Is. 37:36; Exod. 12:29–36).

Hezekiah's sickness also resembles the Passover. His sickness and recovery are a kind of "death and resurrection" (Is. 38:10–11). The angel of death strikes the Assyrians but passes over Hezekiah, who represents the entire nation of Israel.

4. How does Hezekiah's reign end?

Sadly, Hezekiah's reign does not end well. Shortly after he recovers, Hezekiah shows the treasures of the temple to the Babylonians. Isaiah rebukes Hezekiah, but says that judgment will not come in his lifetime. Though Hezekiah recovers from death, his time is short; he lives only fifteen more years. His own life pictures how short Judah's recovery will be. Though the Babylonians leave, they will be back.

5. What does Manasseh's name mean? What does this show about his reign?

Manasseh's name means "Forgetful" and during his reign, Judah is forgetful of God's law and covenant and of Hezekiah's faithfulness. Everything good that Hezekiah did is undone. Manasseh's entire reign is one of "forgetfulness."

6. What does Josiah do during his reign?

Like his grandfather Hezekiah, Josiah cleanses the land of idols, removes the high places, and starts to turn Judah back to the Lord.

7. After Josiah's reign, why is the Lord still angry with Judah?

Even though Josiah is a great king and leads Judah back to the Lord, Yahweh is still angry over the sins of Manasseh (2 Kgs. 23:26–27; 24:4). Zephaniah's prophecy is given during the reign of Josiah (Zeph. 1:1), and it proclaims that a "day of wrath" is on the way.

8. List the kings in the last days of Judah.

Josiah, Jehoiakim, Jehoiachin, and Zedekiah.

THOUGHT QUESTIONS

1. What does the Rabshakeh offer Israel (2 Kgs. 18:31–32)? Explain his offer in the light of God's promises to Israel. How does this add to the blasphemy of the Rabshakeh?

The Rabshakeh offers to take Israel to "a land of grain and new wine, a land of bread and vineyards, a land of olive trees and honey." This offer is a direct challenge to Yahweh. The Rabshakeh is putting himself in the place of Yahweh and is promising Israel all the things that Yahweh promised Israel if they would follow Him. Ultimately, the Rabshakeh is saying that he is the true "god."

2. Discuss the similarities and differences between Josiah and Joash.

Both Joash and Josiah begin their reigns as boys. Both reigns begin with covenant-renewal ceremonies, and both kings go on to purge Judah of her idolatry and reform Judah's worship (2 Kgs. 11–12; 22–23). The main difference is that Joash fell away from the Lord at the end of his life (1 Chr. 24:15–22).

3. Remember that the temple is a picture of Israel. With this in mind, why is there so much emphasis on the temple vessels that Nebuchadnezzar removed from Jerusalem (2 Kgs. 25:13–17; see Dan. 1:1–2)?

They are emphasized because they vividly picture what has happened to Judah. Because Judah refused to repent from serving other gods, Yahweh gave them their desire and sent the temple vessels into the treasury of the gods of Babylon. The temple vessels are like Judah herself, in exile in the house of foreign gods.

4. What is the political situation in Isaiah 7–8? Who is threatening Judah? Why?

Assyria is beginning to rise in the East. The Northern Kingdom of Israel has allied themselves with the Aramean Kingdom and they are pressuring Judah to enter an alliance with Assyria (2 Chr. 28).

5. Isaiah 12:2 quotes from Exodus 15:2. In the context, explain why Isaiah would quote from this song.

The song of Moses in Exodus 15 celebrates the Lord's conquest of the Egyptians during Israel's exodus from Egypt. Isaiah 11–12 looks forward to Israel's restoration after the exile. The quotes from Exodus indicate that Isaiah sees the restoration as a New Exodus.

Another Shiloh: *Jeremiah*

REVIEW QUESTIONS [pages 196–211]

1. What does the vision of the "blown pot" mean?

It means that the Lord is going to send the Babylonians from the north to punish Judah for her idolatry.

2. How is Jeremiah like another Moses? Another Samuel?

Jeremiah reminds us of Moses in many ways. Like Moses, he is reluctant to accept the Lord's call, saying that he cannot speak well (Jer. 1:4–8). As with Moses, the Lord puts His words in the prophet's mouth (Exod. 4:11–16; Deut. 18:18). Moses was the mediator of the covenant at Sinai, and Jeremiah announces a New Covenant that will not fail like the Old Covenant (Jer. 31:27–34).

Jeremiah is also another Samuel (who is, in turn, a new Moses). Like Samuel, he is consecrated from the womb (Jer. 1:5; 1 Sam. 3:1–18). Like Samuel, Jeremiah speaks about the ruin of the sanctuary (1 Sam. 1). Samuel announces judgment not only on Eli and his sons but also on Saul (1 Sam. 13, 15), and Jeremiah advises Zedekiah, who, like Saul, seeks a word from the prophet but turns from those words when things get tough.

3. What event does Jeremiah refer to in his temple sermon in Jeremiah 7? What's the point? Why is it important that Jeremiah delivers this message?

Jeremiah is a prophet from Anathoth, a Levitical city in the tribal land of Benjamin that has become the place where the descendants of Eli are exiled (1 Kgs. 2:26–27). The mention of Anathoth reminds us of the destruction of Yahweh's house in Shiloh. When Jeremiah preaches in the temple, he reminds Judah of what God did at Shiloh and promises that He will do the same with the temple. Judah is repeating the sins of Hophni and Phinehas, and Jeremiah's message is clear: Shiloh is happening all over again.

4. How is Zedekiah like Saul?

Jeremiah's time is like the story of Judah told in reverse (see Jer. 4:23). Solomon's temple has become like Shiloh and Judah's king, Zedekiah, is like Saul; he sides with the people out of fear rather than listens to the world of the prophet (Jer. 38:17–23). Jeremiah also speaks to Zedekiah three times (Jer. 37:3, 17; 38:1–28) in a way that reminds us of Samuel's three interactions with Saul (1 Sam. 13:13–14; 15:17–23; 28).

5. Explain how Jeremiah turns words about the exodus inside out.

When Jeremiah commands Judah to "go out" (Jer. 21:9), which is a direct reference to the Exodus, he means that Judah should follow him in a new Exodus. However, this time Jerusalem is the "Egypt" that the people should leave, and Zekekiah is Pharaoh. Jeremiah's exodus is an exodus *out* of Jerusalem and *into* the hands of Nebuchadnezzar. Life, in this situation, is found by surrender, not conquest.

6. What do the false prophets teach? Explain the confrontation between Jeremiah and Hananiah.

The false prophets that stand against Jeremiah all teach that the Lord will deliver Jerusalem from Nebuchadnezzar. They are trying to heal the nation with lies (Jer. 8:8), lies that everything is okay and that the Lord is pleased with and will protect them. Hananiah is a good example of these false prophets. Hananiah's name means "the Lord is gracious," and his message is in keeping with his name. He maintains that the Lord will never judge Judah because He is so gracious. Rather than accept the yoke of Nebuchadnezzar as Jeremiah insists, Hananiah says that the Lord will break the yoke of Nebuchadnezzar in two years' time. However, because Hananiah and Judah resist the easy yoke offered through Jeremiah, the Lord will put a burdensome yoke of iron on their necks.

7. What does the vision of the baskets of figs mean?

The baskets of figs represent two different groups within Judah (Jer. 2:20–21). The basket of good figs are those who have "gone out" of the land in an exodus into the land of the Chaldeans. God will care for them and ultimately bring them back to be planted in the land. The basket of bad figs are those who remain in Jerusalem under Zedekiah. The Lord takes no pleasure in them and consequently, they will suffer the threefold judgment of sword, famine, and pestilence.

8. How does Jeremiah describe Nebuchadnezzar?

Jeremiah describes Nebuchadnezzar as a New Adam who rules all creation (Jer. 27:1–8). This means that Judah should submit to him and not rebel (v.8).

9. How are the exiles supposed to live? Why?

Jeremiah says that Judah should live in exile peacefully, because the exile will be long, and Babylon's peace means peace and protection for the exiles. Also, Jeremiah says that Israel should build and plant *during* the exile. Babylon will become like the garden-land of Canaan where the Jews will enjoy God's blessing even while outside the land. They are to become Adams and Eves under the great Adamic Emperor Nebuchadnezzar.

10. What does Jeremiah promise will happen after the exile?

While Babylon is a cup of wrath in God's hand, Jeremiah promises that after all the nations have drunk from it, Babylon will herself drink from it too (Jer. 25:26). While they are asleep in a drunken stupor, God will send them away to slaughter (51:39–40). Nebuchadnezzar is a monster who "swallows up" Judah, but like the great fish who swallowed Jonah, he too will vomit Judah back onto dry land.

THOUGHT QUESTIONS

1. What does the prophet warn Judah about in Jeremiah 3:1–5? What is Yahweh preparing to do?

Jeremiah is warning Israel that she cannot continue to play the harlot *and* return to the Lord. Judah has not learned from her adulterous "sister" Israel and has committed the same harlotries without shame. The Lord is threatening to give Judah "a certificate of divorce" just as He gave one to Israel (Jer. 3:6–10).

2. Jesus quotes Jeremiah 7:11 in Matthew 21:13. What is Jesus suggesting by quoting from this passage?

Jesus is saying that the people who worship in the temple of His day are just like their fathers. They put their confidence in the temple and say, "We are delivered" (Jer. 7:8–10). But like their fathers, they profane the temple with their idolatry and evil deeds.

3. Look at Jeremiah 14:19–22. Who does Jeremiah remind you of? How does this fit with larger themes of the book?

This passage reminds us of Moses. Like Moses, Jeremiah pleads with the Lord to remember His people and to save them for His glory's sake. Jeremiah is also a suffering prophet like Moses. He suffers with Judah just as Moses suffered with disobedient Israel in the wilderness for forty years.

4. When is the "New Covenant" in Jeremiah 31:31–34 going to be established? Look at the context.

The context (vv. 23, 27) indicates that the "New Covenant" will be established when Israel is restored from exile.

5. In Jeremiah 38, the prophet is thrown into a pit and then drawn out by Ebed-melech ("servant of the king"), an Ethiopian. This reminds us of Joseph being thrown into the pit and brought out. How are the two incidents similar?

Both incidents end with Joseph and Jeremiah standing before the king, speaking the Lord's word.

CHAPTER 7

EXILE AND NEW EXODUS

Ichabod and Return: *Ezekiel 8–11, 40–48*

REVIEW QUESTIONS [pages 215–222]

1. Where was Ezekiel when he was prophesying? What was happening in Jerusalem at the same time?

Ezekiel was taken to Babylon after Nebuchadnezzar's second invasion of Judah. He prophesied in Babylon at the same time Jeremiah was prophesying in Jerusalem, and while Zedekiah was king in Jerusalem.

2. What was Ezekiel's first vision?

Ezekiel's first vision is of the "glory cloud" of God's presence (Exod. 40:34–38; 1 Kgs. 8:10–11). In his vision, the cloud leaves Jerusalem and goes with the exiles into Babylon because of Judah's idolatry. Though they are cut off from the temple, the Jews in Babylon are not cut off from the presence of the Lord. They are the "good figs" of Jeremiah's vision. They are going to be the beginning of a "new creation."

3. What does Ezekiel see in the temple?

In his vision Ezekiel sees what is happening behind the scenes in the Temple. The walls are covered with "every form of creeping things and beasts and detestable things, with all the idols of the house of Israel," and the seventy elders of

Israel are offering incense to the idols (8:11–12). Ezekiel sees women weeping for Tammuz, a Babylonian god (vv. 14–15). In the inner court, the High Priest and the heads of the twenty-four priestly clans set up by David are bowing east toward the sunrise, the direction of exile (vv. 16–18).

4. What is the Lord planning to do to the people of the city?

The Lord is planning to destroy the city. Instead of guarding Jerusalem, the Lord is attacking it. Only those who "sigh and groan over all the abominations" of Jerusalem will be saved (9:3–4).

5. What is important about the phrase "that they may know that I am the Lord"?

This repeated phrase comes from the book of Exodus where Yahweh sends plagues on Pharaoh so that he might know who the God of Israel is (Exod. 5:2). However, in Ezekiel it is *Judah* who is saying, "Who is Yahweh? I don't know Yahweh." So the Lord is sending the plagues of Egypt on His own people so that they might know who He is.

6. After his wife's death, in what way is Ezekiel silent? Why?

The death of Ezekiel's wife is symbolic of the fall of the sanctuary, and Ezekiel is told to observe the High Priest's rules for mourning (Ezek. 24:16–18; cf. Lev. 21:10–12). Similarly, he is also told to be silent until "that day" when the city and the temple finally fall (Ezek. 24:27). Though he is silent toward Judah and the exiles, Ezekiel sends messages to seven Gentile nations (chs. 25–32), which are meant to provoke Judah to jealousy.

7. What is the vision in Ezekiel 37 about?

The vision of the "dry bones" is about resurrection from the death of exile. The Lord will "open your graves and cause you to come out of your graves, My people; and I will bring you into the land of Israel" (37:11–12). Moreover, Israel died a divided nation; they are raised a reunited nation (37:19–22).

8. How is the story that Ezekiel tells like the story of the Exodus and conquest?

The final chapters of Ezekiel (36–48) describe Israel's return from exile in a way that reminds us of the Exodus and conquest. Israel comes out of a Gentile land and enters her own land (chs. 36–37); she fights with and defeats the nations (chs. 38–39); then she builds a house and divides the land (chs. 40–48).

9. How does Ezekiel show us that the city of Jerusalem is a holy city?

Ezekiel describes the temple as if it was a city (40:2). The subsequent measurements (vv. 12–17) indicate that Jerusalem as a whole has become holy space, since only holy places feature exact dimensions. The city's name (v. 35) means that the city is holy because the Lord dwells there.

10. How does the temple revive the land?

The new holy house/city of the Lord makes the whole land clean and fruitful. In chapter 47, water flows from the temple toward the east. The water grows deeper and deeper and restores the land and sea. The water from the temple turns the land back into an "Eden."

THOUGHT QUESTIONS

1. Ezekiel sees a man in linen enter the cherubim cloud and get a handful of coals, which he scatters over the city (Ezek. 10:1–2). Compare to Exodus 9:8–12 and Revelation 8:3–5 and explain the parallels between the passages.

All three passages show that the imagery of scattering ash/coals is a judgment.

2. Who are the ones who plaster the walls with "whitewash" (Ezek. 13:8–16)?

They are the false prophets who say "Peace!" when there is no peace. This combination of whitewashing and speaking lies also reminds us of Jesus' words to the Pharisees in Matthew 23:27.

3. Explain the allegories in Ezekiel 16 and 23. How is Judah pictured?

In Ezekiel 16 and 23, Judah is pictured as the harlot bride who has left her Husband and has "spread her legs" to lovers from other nations. The bottom line is that Judah has completely abandoned her Husband and has prostituted herself with other gods. In chapter 23, Judah is imitating the idolatry/harlotries of her "sister" Israel (Oholah).

4. Look at Ezekiel 33:30–33. How is this passage like Matthew 11:17?

In Matthew 11:17, Jesus is likening His generation to the people of Ezekiel's time. Both were willing to "listen to the music," but neither were willing to respond appropriately—that is, with obedience.

5. What is the purpose of Ezekiel's description of the temple (43:10–12)? Explain how he accomplishes this purpose.

The purpose of Ezekiel's description of the temple is to cause the Israelites to "be ashamed of their iniquity" (43:10). The picture of the temple with walls that are "square" and "straight" is meant to be a picture of Israel and her faithfulness to Yahweh's commands. Israel, however, is a "crooked" house, and the vision of the temple reveals her faithlessness and calls her to repentance.

Times of Gentiles: *Daniel*
From Zealot to Witness: *Esther*

REVIEW QUESTIONS [pages 223–229]

1. Give some examples of how Daniel stays faithful to the Lord while in exile.

In exile, Daniel serves the Lord even when it means that he must disobey the king of Babylon. Every time this happens, however, Yahweh saves Daniel and promotes him. When Daniel refuses the king's food (1:14–15), Yahweh causes him to become stronger than the other men (1:19–20). When Daniel interprets Nebuchadnezzar's dream, the king praises God and raises Daniel up to a new position (2:47–49). When Daniel refuses to pray to Darius, Yahweh not only spares Daniel's life but also causes the king to praise the God of Israel (6:26–27).

2. What happens when Daniel and his friends obey God?

Because Daniel and his friends follow Jeremiah's words and seek the peace of Babylon, the Lord protects and prospers them there and causes the Gentile king to praise His power (Dan. 6:26–27).

3. How do the stories of Daniel picture God's promises to the exiles in Babylon?

The stories of Daniel reaffirm Yahweh's words through Jeremiah to go peacefully to Babylon, accept the discipline of the Lord, and be a faithful witness before the Gentiles. If the Jews seek the peace and welfare of Babylon, they will be saved from all their enemies, and kings of the earth will marvel at the power of Yahweh.

4. What are Daniel's visions about the "times of the Gentiles"? What message does this send to the exiles?

Daniel's visions show that a new world has come, a world in which Israel will not be a separate nation but will be under a Gentile world empire. However, Daniel's visions also show that the Gentile nations will not rule forever. They will be replaced by a kingdom that "the God of heaven will set up," and this kingdom is one that "will never be destroyed" (Dan. 2:36–45; 7:13–22, 27). Daniel's visions teach Israel patience during exile—she must wait for the Lord to come set up His kingdom.

5. At the beginning of Esther, is Mordecai a faithful man? Why or why not?

In the opening chapters of Esther, Mordecai is a compromised character who seeks influence and exaltation by encouraging Esther to hide the fact that she is a Jew. Unlike Daniel who rises to power because he is unwilling to compromise, Mordecai is seeking to become powerful by compromising with the Persians.

6. Is Mordecai right when he refuses to bow before Haman?

Rather than being faithful as Daniel was, Mordecai "makes a show" of his faithfulness by foolishly refusing to bow to Haman and thus disobeying the order of the king (Est. 3:1–2). Mordecai's pride endangered the entire Jewish nation (3:8).

7. Who is Haman? Why is this significant?

Haman is an Agagite. Agag was the king of the Amalekites who fought against Saul. God had commanded that the Amalekites were to be utterly destroyed, but Israel failed to carry out the command fully. The battle between Mordecai (a descendant of Benjamin, like Saul) and Haman is the final battle in Yahweh's war against the Amalekites.

8. Give some examples of the Lord acting to save His people in the book of Esther.

Haman's lot, resulting in a "delayed" date to attack the Jews; the king's willingness to receive Esther (5:1–4); and the final reversal of Haman's plot to hang Mordecai all show the Lord at work "behind the scenes" to protect and save His people.

9. What is the message of Esther to the exiles?

If the exiles will repent and confess the Lord among the Gentiles, Yahweh will exalt them and give them victory. He will also make the Gentiles turn to Him in fear (8:17).

THOUGHT QUESTIONS

1. What is Belshazzar doing on the night that Babylon is taken by the Persians (Dan. 5:1–9)? Why?

He is having a feast. This isn't just a case of "fiddling while Rome burns": Belshazzar is holding a religious feast, using Yahweh's temple vessels, in order to call the gods of Babylon to his aid.

2. Daniel 9:24–27 contains the famous "seventy weeks" prophecy. When does the period of "seventy weeks" begin? When does it end?

The "seventy weeks" begins with Cyrus' decree to rebuild Jerusalem. The last week is difficult to interpret, but it is referring to the "cutting off" of the Messiah and the "abomination of desolations" (Dan. 9:26–27). The prophecies point to Jesus' death and resurrection and the destruction of the temple in 70 A.D. (Mt. 24:1–28), and not to the re-founding of Israel in 1948 as some assume.

3. Look at the uses of the phrase "latter days" in Daniel 2:28 and 10:14. When do the "latter days" begin?

According to these passages, the "latter days" begin with Nebuchadnezzar and continue through to the destruction of the temple in A.D. 70.

4. Compare Esther 5:11 with 1:4. What does this suggest about Haman's view of his own prestige?

It suggests that Haman thinks of himself as a "king" like Ahasuerus.

5. Explain how the feasts provide a structure for the story in Esther.

Esther is structured around seven feasts that culminate in the feast of Purim. The number seven reminds us of the creation week. In Esther, Yahweh "remakes" His people and gives them rest from their enemies.

Second Exodus: *Ezra and Nehemiah*

REVIEW QUESTIONS [pages 229–238]

1. To what does Isaiah compare the return from Babylon?

Isaiah says that Israel's return from Babylon will be an event even greater than the Exodus (Is. 11:15–16). Moreover, it will be so great that it will make Israel forget about her deliverance from Egypt (43:14–21). The return from exile will be a new creation (44:24–28) in which exilic "death" is vanquished by resurrection "life."

2. Explain some of the similarities between the return from Babylon and the Exodus.

As in the Exodus, Israel "plunders" the Persians (Ezra 1:6) and Babylonians. As Israel used the plunder of Egypt to build the tabernacle, now she uses the plunder of Persia to rebuild the temple. Ezra 2 is also like a miniature book of Numbers that records the people who return in the "Exodus" from Babylon.

3. Explain some of the differences between the first and second exodus.

In the first Exodus, Pharaoh let Israel go only after being crushed by the devastating plagues; Cyrus lets Israel go freely and gives them permission to rebuild the Lord's house. The Egyptians give gold and silver to Israel because the fear of God had fallen on them; the Persians give their wealth to Israel as a freewill offering. Because Israel has repented of her hostility to the Gentile empire, there is now goodwill between Israel and the Gentiles. Finally, the new Exodus is not accompanied by the same signs that marked Israel's departure from Egypt. God is now guiding Israel less by miracles and more through the teachers of Israel as Jeremiah promises (Jer. 31:27–34).

4. What are the different stages in rebuilding the house of God?

First, the Jews, under the oversight of Joshua and Zerubbabel, build an altar, offer sacrifices, and celebrate the feasts of Israel (Neh. 3:1–5). The second task is to rebuild the temple itself, a task which is eventually postponed by Darius (Ezra 4:1–24), but is completed at the urging of Haggai and Zechariah (Ezra 5:1–2).

5. What is Haggai's prophecy about?

Haggai rebukes the Jews for diverting their energies from building the temple to the construction of their own homes. The Lord's house is in ruins, and the Lord will bring ruin on Israel in response (Hag. 1:1–11).

6. What is Zechariah's prophecy about? What does the vision of Joshua in filthy garments mean?

Zechariah is concerned that Israel repent and "return" to the Lord with all their heart. He reminds them that their fathers were overtaken by the curse of the covenant because they did not "turn" when the prophets warned them.

Zechariah's vision of Joshua in filthy garments shows that Joshua is a defiled High Priest who can't serve in the Lord's house, and thus cannot help Israel. Moreover, without a temple Joshua can't offer a sacrifice to make himself clean. In this hopeless situation, the Lord tells His angels to put clean clothes on Joshua (Zech. 3:4–5) so that he can be restored to his position as High Priest.

7. What is Ezra's job? How is this related to rebuilding the Lord's "house"?

Ezra is a priest (Ezra 7:5) and an expert in the law of Moses (7:6) whose responsibility is to study the law and teach it to Israel (7:10). By doing this, Ezra is building the house of Israel, which is the house of God. He is also ensuring the cleanliness of the temple *by* teaching the people to observe the law of God.

8. What is Nehemiah's job? How is this related to rebuilding the Lord's "house"?

Nehemiah is responsible for rebuilding the walls of Jerusalem. Building the walls of the city is part of building the temple because the holy city is part of the Lord's house. This is why Nehemiah "dedicates" the walls to the Lord as "holy" (Neh. 12:27).

THOUGHT QUESTIONS

1. What does Cyrus say about the Lord in his decree (Ezra 1:1–4)? What does this suggest about Cyrus?

Cyrus confesses that Yahweh is the God of heaven. He also says that Yahweh has given him his authority and has commanded him to build His temple. It suggests that Cyrus has become a "God-fearing" Gentile. As Peter Leithart has said, "Be ready to make Cyrus's acquaintance when you get to the new heavens and earth."

2. The story of Ezra's return from Babylon includes details of the treasures that Ezra is bringing (Ezra 7:11–26; 8:24–30). Why?

Israel's return from Babylon is an Exodus story, and they "plunder" the Persians just as they did the Egyptians, only this time the Persians give their gifts freely.

3. In Ezra 9:1, the princes tell Ezra that the people are marrying Canaanites, Hittites, and so on. Many of these people no longer live in the land. Why do the princes call the people of the land by these names?

Ezra is applying the law to a new situation, and he classifies the people as "Canaanites" even though they ethnically are not. By doing so, Ezra is reminding Israel of their unfaithful history (being like the Canaanites) and is warning them of the danger of intermarriage leading to idolatry.

4. Nehemiah has to deal with conflicts between Jews (Neh. 5:1–13). What are they fighting about? What laws are they violating?

They are arguing over the practice of usury among the Israelites. They were disregarding the commands of Leviticus 25:35–46, which required Israel to care for the poor. Specifically, they were not allowed to charge a brother interest and they were not to subject him to a slave's service (vv. 36, 39).

5. What proportion of the Jews live in Jerusalem after the exile (Neh. 11:1–2)? Why?

One tenth of the Jews that leave Babylon are chosen to live in Jerusalem. They are a "tithe" given to the city because it is holy.

CHAPTER 8

ISRAEL DEAD AND REBORN

The Greater Jeremiah, the Greater Solomon
Jesus Among the Jews

REVIEW QUESTIONS [pages 241–249]

1. In what ways is Jesus like Jeremiah?

Like Jeremiah, Jesus is a prophet who warns Israel that her sins will soon cause the Lord to destroy His house. Like John the Baptist, Jesus warns that "the kingdom of heaven is at hand" and that "the axe is laid at the foot of the tree" (Lk. 3:7–9).

2. What does Jesus mean when He warns about judgment against "this generation"?

Jesus' clearest teaching about the judgment to come is recorded in Matthew 24. He prophesies that a great judgment is going to come on "this generation" because they are rejecting Him, God's greatest prophet. When Jesus speaks about "this generation," He is talking about the Jews who are living in Judea and Jerusalem during His lifetime. He is saying that before "this generation" passes away Jerusalem and the temple are going to be destroyed. Shiloh is about to happen all over again.

3. Who are the "Jews" in John's gospel? How does John emphasize Jesus' conflict with them?

Occasionally John uses the term "Jew" to refer to all who follow the Mosaic law (cf. 12:9–11), but most of the time "Jew" refers to the rulers and leaders of Israel who live in Jerusalem and who hate Jesus (see 9:22; 18:3, 12; 8:13, 18ff). Since these leaders represent the nation, the "Jews" as a people reject Jesus when their leaders do.

4. What does John teach us by reminding us of creation in chapter one of his gospel?

He is telling us that Jesus' coming is the beginning of a new creation.

5. How does John foreshadow the conflicts between Jesus and the Jews in chapter one of John? How are the Jews "darkness"?

In the midst of this new creation, John says, there is conflict: the darkness is trying to "overcome" the light (1:5). The Jews are that darkness because they cling to the "old" creation once the light of God's new creation in Jesus has been revealed. Being in darkness is not a sin—the sin is for darkness to seek to overpower the Light instead of giving way to the Light. The sin is to love shadows rather than the reality.

6. What happens to the blind man that Jesus heals? How is this a preview of what happens later in the New Testament?

The blind man Jesus heals has been blind from birth, and his healing is a "new birth." Jesus "remakes" the blind man into a new "Adam" by putting clay on his eyes, just as Yahweh breathed on dust to make Adam (Jn. 9:6). Immediately following his "rebirth," the man is put on trial by the Pharisees and is ultimately cast out of the synagogue. This becomes a pattern for those who are "born again" in Jesus—they are put on trial and cast out of the synagogue.

7. Why are some of the Jews afraid to confess Jesus openly?

Fear of the Jews' ability to "cast out" also keeps some rulers from following Jesus. They would rather have honor from men than honor from God (Jn. 12:42–43).

8. Why do some of Jesus' disciples leave Him? What does Jesus think of this?

Some of Jesus' followers stop following Him when things get difficult. Some find Jesus' words about eating His flesh and drinking His blood offensive (Jn. 6:66). Others, trusting in their blood connection to Abraham, are offended by Jesus' claim to be greater than Abraham (8:31–59). This is the context of Jesus' strongest attack against the "Jews" (vv. 39–47). Here the "Jews" refer to those who believe in Him but turn aside from following Him. They are not of Jesus, but are of their father, the devil.

9. What are the Jews afraid of after the raising of Lazarus?

After Lazarus is raised, many of the Jews believe in Jesus (Jn. 12:9–11). This makes the Jewish leaders fear that Rome will get involved and take away their "place" (the temple) and "nation" (11:48).

10. What city is destroyed in Revelation?

In Revelation the city's name is "Sodom and Egypt" (Rev. 11:8) and "Babylon the Great" (17:5). These mystical names are identified with the city "where also their Lord was crucified" (11:8), Jerusalem. Because Jerusalem has rejected the Messiah, she has become more like Sodom, Egypt, and Babylon than the city of God.

THOUGHT QUESTIONS

1. How does the miracle of healing in John 4:46–54 fit with the conflict between Jesus and the Jews?

The official at Capernaum is a rebuke to his own people because, while the Jews "see" the signs that Jesus performs and refuse to believe, the official believes that Jesus has healed son even when he can't see it. The difference, of course, is faith. The official believes in Jesus and is granted the eyes to "see" what the other Jews cannot see (Jn. 9:39).

2. Whom does Jesus call as His "witnesses" in John 5:19–47?

Here Jesus calls the Jews to the witness of John (vv. 33–35), the witness of His works (v. 36), the witness of the Father (vv. 37–38), and the witness of the Scripture (vv. 39–47).

3. What do the Jews plot to do after Jesus raises Lazarus (Jn. 11:53–57)? How does this fit with the theme introduced in 1:5?

Jesus withdrew from "walking publicly among the Jews" because the leaders of Israel had plotted to seize and then kill Him. Again, the Jews are pictured as the darkness trying to overcome the Light of the world.

4. Why do the people think that Jesus is a "prophet" when He feeds the five thousand (6:14)? See 2 Kings 4:42–44.

In 2 Kings 4:42–44, Elisha divides twenty loaves of bread and heads of fresh grain to feed the people. Jesus' actions remind the people of Elisha.

Grace and Truth Through Jesus

REVIEW QUESTIONS [pages 250–258]

1. How does Jesus' miracle at the wedding feast show that He is better than Moses?

In Exodus 7:19, Moses changes the water of Egypt into blood, including the water in the wood and stone waterpots. For Moses, this is the first sign against Pharaoh and Egypt. Jesus, the greater Moses, does not perform a sign of judgment but a sign of blessing, changing water to the blood of grapes.

2. Why is it important that John tells about Jesus cleansing the temple at the beginning of His gospel?

John wants us to see Jesus' whole ministry as an effort to "cleanse" the house of God. Jesus brings the worship of the temple to a halt for a few minutes as a sign of what was to happen to "this generation." He is warning the Jews about what would happen if they refused to repent and believe in Him.

3. Explain the symbolism of the miracle that healed the man at the pool. How does this show Jesus is greater than Moses?

By this time in John's gospel, we know that water is a picture of the old order that Jesus comes to fulfill and replace. This water cannot make men acceptable sacrifices. Only the word of the Jesus does this. Jesus comes to the broken sheep of Israel to give them abundant life. The Mosaic order of water and purification cannot heal. Jesus can. Jesus heals a man who has been sick for thirty-eight years, the same amount of time that Israel is in the wilderness and cannot pass into the land. The man's problem is that he cannot go throught the waters. He is stuck in the wilderness. The Mosaic system cannot take him into the land, just as Moses himself does not enter. To pass through the waters to new life, the man needs a Joshua. And Joshua (Jesus) comes to him. Jesus takes him out the wilderness, makes him suitable as a sacrifice, and raises him from Old Covenant death to New Covenant life.

4. How does John 6 follow the Passover-Exodus story?

During the time of Passover, Jesus offers a new Passover feast to those who gather with Him on the mountain. After the Passover feast, Jesus crosses the sea and saves His disciples from the storm, which is like a new exodus. Following this exodus, Jesus greets the gathering crowds in a wilderness scene and, instead of giving manna, Jesus offers Himself as the "bread of heaven." In all of this Jesus is presented as the greater Moses.

5. In what ways is Jesus' sermon in John 13–17 like Deuteronomy?

In John 13–17, Jesus gives a "farewell" sermon that mirrors Moses' final sermons to Israel in Deuteronomy. Just as Moses reminded Israel of the laws and commandments they were to obey when they entered the Promised Land, so Jesus tells His disciples that they must obey His commandments. Deuteronomy also speaks about Israel's future conquest of the Promised Land; likewise, Jesus talks about the future of His people. As Moses was replaced by Joshua, Jesus tells His disciples that, though He is going away, He will send another "Joshua," the Holy Spirit, to comfort them and lead them in the conquest of the world.

6. Who is "the world" in John 13–17? How do you know?

When Jesus speaks about "the world" in these chapters, He is referring to the Jews. We know this because Jesus tells the disciples that just as "the world" hated and persecuted Him, so "it" will do the same to them (15:18–16:4). In John 15:20, Jesus says that if "they" persecute Me, they will persecute you. In 5:16, we are told that the Jews persecute Jesus because He heals the lame. In 15:21, Jesus says that "they" do not know the One who sent Him, and this is said about the Jews earlier in the gospel. In 8:19, Jesus says the Jews do not know Him or His Father and repeats in 8:55 that the Jews have not come to know Him. In 15:24–16:4, it becomes even clearer that Jesus is talking about the Jews. He speaks of "their law" (16:2), warns that "they will make you outcasts from the synagogue," and predicts that "everyone who kills you will think that he is offering service to God."

7. What does Jesus say "the world" will do?

After Jesus' hour, "the world" (the Jews) will have their hour and will persecute the disciples and "make you outcasts from the synagogue." The Jews are "the world" that is hostile to Jesus and His church.

8. What effect will the Spirit have on "the world"?

In John 16:7–11, Jesus speaks of the Spirit's effect on the "world." The Spirit will convict the Jews who have renounced their Lord and ultimately bring about a revival among them.

THOUGHT QUESTIONS

1. To what is Jesus comparing Himself in 1:51?

Jesus likens Himself to the ladder in Jacob's vision at Bethel. Jesus is the one who unites heaven and earth; He is "Beth-el" (House of God). In Colossians 1:13–20, Christ is the one who reconciles all things, whether in heaven or on earth, to the Father.

2. John calls Jesus' miracles "signs" (see 2:11; 4:48). Explain this term in light of Exodus 7:3.

The "signs" of Exodus 7:3 are judgments against Pharaoh's hardness of heart. Similarly, John sees Jesus' miracles as "signs" of judgment against the Jews' hardness of heart. It also indicates that Israel has become Egypt and is ripe for judgment.

3. Who dug the well where Jesus stops in Samaria (Jn. 4:12)? Why is this significant?

Jacob dug the well in Samaria. Jesus' interaction with the woman at the well shows that He is the greater Jacob. Jacob provided water for his people, but Jesus provides "living" water. Jesus is Jacob's greater Son.

Like Isaac, He is a bridegroom, looking for His bride at the well of His father, and His bride is going to include people like the Samaritans (Gentiles). This Bridegroom brings a better covenant than His father Jacob.

4. In light of the meaning of "the world" in John 13–17, what does John 3:16 mean?

In John 13–17, the apostle uses the phrase "the world" to refer to the Jews. John 3:16 is pointedly saying that God so loved the very people who hated and rejected Him. He was willing to give His only Begotten Son for their salvation.

5. When does Jesus "come" to His disciples (Jn. 14:18)? Look closely at the context.

The context suggests that Jesus understands His "coming" to His disciples as His presence with them through the gift of His Spirit on Pentecost.

A King in Israel: *John 18–19*

REVIEW QUESTIONS [pages 259–263]

1. How does John describe the "hour" of Jesus?

John describes Jesus' hour as "judgment of this world" (12:31). His point is to emphasize that though the crucifixion seems to be a judgment on Jesus, it is actually a judgment on the Jews.

2. Explain the arrangement of the trial before Pilate. How many scenes are there? How are the scenes marked off from one another?

John emphasizes that Jesus' trial before Pilate is Jesus' trial as the king of the Jews. In John 18:28–19:16, Jesus is called "king" eleven times. The trial is divided into seven scenes. Each scene is divided from one another by Pilate's movements into and out of the Praetorium.

3. What is at the center of the story? What are the soldiers doing?

The central scene is when the solders whip and mock Jesus. The soldiers perform a mock coronation, pretending to crown Jesus king of the Jews. They crown Him with thorns, cover Him with a purple robe, and bring Him out to the people to be acclaimed as king (Jn. 19:1–6). But instead of receiving Him as their king, the Jews shout out, "Crucify Him, crucify Him!"

4. Explain the double sense of the word that tells us that Pilate "sat down" in the judgment seat.

The Greek verb for "sat down" can also mean "cause to sit." Because of this it is unclear whether Pilate sat down or whether he made Jesus sit down on the judgment seat. It further raises the question of who is really in charge of "judging." Though Jesus appears to be on trial, John's answer is that Jesus is really presiding at the trial.

5. How is the trial of Jesus the trial of the Jews?

Jesus' trial is a repeat of the times of Samuel. Israel is being tested about whether she will accept Yahweh as her king. As in Samuel's time, Israel rejects Yahweh and wants to be just like the other nations. They say, "We have no king but Caesar" (Jn. 19:15). And that is exactly what they get.

6. What is significant about the "stone pavement"?

In the Old Testament, the Greek word for "stone pavement" is used only a couple of times. Significantly, in 2 Chronicles 7:1–3, after Solomon finishes his temple, the glory of the Lord fills the house. When the Lord takes His throne in the temple, Israel bows down on the "pavement" with her face to the ground and praises her King. But here in Pilate's Praetorium, Jesus is seated as the Word of God incarnate, the Glory of God, the Judge of Israel, before a stone pavement. And the Jews renounce Him. They do not fall on the stone pavement before their king, and so the stone will fall on them and grind them to power.

THOUGHT QUESTIONS

1. What is significant about the Jews' choice of Barabbas (Jn. 18:38–40)?

In choosing Barabbas, Israel is siding with a revolutionary rather than the Prince of Peace, and their disastrous future reflects their choice. Second, Barabbas's name means "son of the father," so Israel is choosing one "son" over another.

2. When Jesus is pierced in the side, blood and water come out (Jn. 19:34). How is this connected with Jesus' statements in 4:13–14 and 7:37–39?

The water that flows from Jesus' side is like the water that flows from the temple in Ezekiel 47 and the water that flows from the garden of Eden (Gen. 3:10–14). Calvary is a new Eden and the living water that flows from Jesus' side gives life to the whole world. Jesus' disciples who drink of the living water become part of the temple of Jesus' body and from their "innermost being" water flows to all vivify all creation.

3. Discuss the scene in John 20:11–18 in light of Genesis 2:18–25.

John draws on the imagery of Genesis 2:18–25 to describe Jesus as a new Adam. Just as Adam goes into a deep sleep and awakens to meet his bride in the garden, so Jesus arises from His "sleep" of death and meets His bride (represented by Mary) in a garden. Further, Mary mistakes Jesus for "the gardener," another echo of Jesus as the new Adam. All of this shows that Jesus' resurrection is the beginning of a New Creation.

4. When Peter sees Jesus on the beach after the resurrection, Jesus is at a charcoal fire (Jn. 21:9). Why? See John 18:18.

The last time we saw Peter at a charcoal fire, he was denying Jesus. That fire was in the high priest's court where Peter chose to deny Jesus three times. In John 21:12, the fire reminds us of Peter's betrayal, but now Jesus restores Peter to his "hearth" and feeds him.

CPSIA information can be obtained
at www.ICGtesting.com
Printed in the USA
BVHW041108180619
551193BV00014B/191/P